Rosemary L

PIONUS PA

best wishes,
Sharon

Rosemary Low

dona

ACKNOWLELDGEMENTS

The author wishes to thank Olivier Arnoult, Armin Brockner, Nigel Harcourt-Brown FRCVS and Roger Sweeney for replying to requests for information, also the breeders whose experiences are quoted. Information on status in the wild was obtained from *Handbook of the Birds of the World*, volume 4.
All photographs were taken by the author at Loro Parque, Tenerife, except the Maximilan's and White-crowned Pionus which are privately owned. The photograph of *Pionus sordidus mindoensis* was taken by Armin Brockner.

ISBN 80-7322-005-9

Contents

Introduction

Pionus are a genus of small to medium-sized parrots from South and Central America. Their shape is similar to that of Amazon parrots; they have solid bodies and short, wide tails. They are smaller than Amazons. Their "trade mark" is the red under tail coverts. This term needs to be explained. It is not the underside of the tail as such but the almost triangular-shaped patch of feathers below the vent. They are scarlet and make a wonderful contrast to the rest of the plumage. Pionus are unusual among parrots in that in some of the seven species the head appears speckled with white; little tufts of down produce this effect; it is perfectly natural. These parrots vary in length from 28cm (11in) to only about 24 cm (9in to 10in) and in weight from about 250g to 180g.

Their advantage from the avicultural viewpoint is that they are not as noisy as most other neotropical parrots. They make engaging pets and aviary birds. An aviculturist who decided to specialise in this group would have not, as in most other genera of neotropical parrots (except macaws), aviaries full of green birds, but an exciting array of colours. Some species are basically green, two are mainly dark blue and bronze, and one is uniquely and variably coloured in shades of brown with touches of blue, white and pink.

This book is designed as an introduction to this attractive group of parrots, as companions and as aviary birds. It also provides a little information about how they live in the wild. Hopefully it will awake an interest in a group of parrots that is sometimes overlooked in favour of their better known cousins, the Amazons.

Note that the noun parrot can be used in the common name in place of the word Pionus. I have used the one that is most commonly used in avicultural circles, eg, White-crowned Pionus, rather than White-crowned Parrot. Where there is a common name in smaller type, this is the name used in ornithological publications.

Chapter 1

Care and housing

The behaviour and characteristics of Pionus parrots are fairly close to those of Amazons. The behaviour of the seven species of Pionus does not vary significantly among the different members of the genus, except in the smallest member, the White- crowned. Some species appear to be very closely related. The immature plumage is a clue to this fact as in that stage, several are quite close to Maximilian's in appearance. I suspect that the latter was the ancestral form.

As Pionus are not as noisy, people with close neighbours will find them a more suitable alternative to their large and more vocal "cousins". The aviaries can therefore be situated near the house. This is an obvious advantage from the aspect of security. In addition, you will obtain more pleasure from your birds if you can see at least some of them from your house. Pionus parrots are inquisitive and will derive as much interest from watching you as you do from observing them.

Housing

Before you start work on aviary construction you need to decide on the floor surface. If it will be concrete, you need drains and a soakaway. This is especially important with Pionus because they do not do well in cool, damp conditions. The soakaway makes cleaning with a pressure washer simple; it also prevents water staying on the surface after heavy rain. Installing drains and a soakaway is initially more time-consuming and expensive but their existence will create a more hygienic environment. As Pionus parrots are susceptible to aspergillosis, this has important health benefits in the long term. The alternative is scrubbing concrete – not a pleasant task!

If the area to be concreted is not large, you can place the drainpipe in the centre of the concrete base, or in the centre of the service passage. It is very important to slope the concrete steeply enough to allow the water to run into the drain; if this is not done, it will lie on the concrete surface. The first step is to create the soakaway, which should extend several feet outside the perimeter of the base. Lay the pipes at a depth of about 1.2m (4ft) below where the concrete surface will be, dig a soakaway, cover it in a ton of gravel, then place a plastic sheet on top to prevent the soakaway filling up. Put the earth back on top of the sheet.

The alternative is a floor made of shingle (small stones). You can buy them from a builder's merchant; ask for 20mm (4/5in gravel). For an aviary 4.5m (15ft) long and 91cm (3ft) wide, you will need half a ton. It is easy to keep clean by hosing it or with a pressure washer. Another possible option is laying paving slabs. An earth floor is not suitable. It cannot be cleaned or disinfected and will pose the enormous problem of letting in mice and rats. They eat the birds' food and carry disease, possibly with fatal results to the aviary occupants.

The best material for the aviary framework is aluminium angle. Wood is difficult to keep clean, it has a limited life because it rots or is gnawed away by the Pionus, and needs to be treated with a preservative every few years. Aluminium angle is maintenance free and always looks smart.

In a block of aviaries each one should be double-wired. If this precaution is not taken, fighting with neighbouring birds will occur. This results in injured feet and even the upper mandible of a bird's beak ripped off. Newly fledged young are especially vulnerable to such injuries, as they are not aware of the dangers posed by aggressive neighbours.

It is very important to use the right type of welded mesh in the aviary construction. The most common mistake is to use mesh that is too large or too thin. For Pionus I would recommend the use of 14g (2mm) welded mesh, 1.25cm (1/2in) square. Make sure the welded mesh is of good quality. Ingestion of loose flakes of zinc found in cheap mesh can kill parrots.

I find the trend towards keeping Pionus in aviaries or cages only 2m (6ft) long disturbing. In my opinion, in order to exercise properly they need an aviary at least 3m (10ft) long. They might be inactive in a smaller aviary, making little or no attempt to fly.

In an outdoor aviary, Pionus need a fully enclosed shelter or a cage or a flight inside an enclosed building. They need this as protection against severe weather conditions. The option to shut them inside at night is one that will increase their lifespan. They will not be vulnerable to attacks by nocturnal predators, or to disturbance from lights of cars and neighbouring houses (including security lights). I feel this is much more important for Pionus than, for example, for Amazon Parrots, as Pionus are more easily stressed.

One consideration when building aviaries for Pionus is a misting (spray) system. They love to become thoroughly drenched. Most species come from areas of high humidity. The installation of pipes running along the top of the aviaries, with the nozzle at the top or, for suspended aviaries, at the side, is a good method of providing a fine spray. Garden centres sell the necessary equipment. The spray system can be attached to a timer. However, unless there is a drain and soakaway in aviaries with solid floors the misting system could create excessive damp.

Although a degree of humidity is necessary, in an enclosed building it can be lethal because it creates permanent damp. The owner of a pair of Bronze-winged Pionus in the north of England decided to give extra protection to the small aviary they inhabited during a severe winter. Normally the sides of the aviary were covered in Perspex during the colder months. That year, however, he covered the entire aviary (only 2m long and 1.2m wide) in Perspex. The resulting condensation and lack of ventilation were blamed for the respiratory infection that the pair developed. Unfortunately, both birds died (Anon, 1997a). The pair had been treated with antibiotics some months previously for a severe *E. coli* infection, so might not have been in the best of health, although they had produced two chicks that year. However, it is likely that the damp environment was to blame for their demise. This story should act as a warning regarding the importance of adequate ventilation.

The type of aviary to be built will depend on climatic conditions. These birds must be protected from damp cold and from strong winds. They are usually cold hardy, except when very young; it is the combination of cold and damp that is so harmful. In a warm climate suspended cages, if of adequate length, will be satisfactory. Attention must be paid to cleanliness because Pionus are susceptible to fungal infections. Fungus spores from mouldy food on the aviary floor can spell death. Food quickly goes mouldy in warm, damp weather. Even if the whole aviary is not cleaned out, priority should be given to daily removal of fruits and vegetables that fall on to the aviary floor. Mould can also form on droppings, so these must be moved frequently in damp, warm weather. In dry weather, some accumulation of droppings should not be harmful.

If your Pionus is a companion bird, kept in the house, you should provide the largest cage you can afford or, better still, a small indoor aviary. The location should be near a window as parrots like to see what is going on outside, but not in direct sunlight. A corner of the room is the best place, as it gives the parrot a feeling of security.

Chapter 2

Diet and nutrition

Perhaps the most important advice that can be given to Pionus owners is to ensure that their birds ingest sufficient Vitamin A. This helps them to fight infections, especially those of the respiratory system, to which Pionus are so susceptible. It is very sad that many Pionus die after only three or four years because the owner is unaware of this vitally important aspect. I believe that the main reason why few Pionus lived to a good age in the past was due to malnutrition. This should alter, now that it is so much easier to provide them with a balanced diet or with vitamin and mineral additives.

There are two methods of trying to provide Pionus with a balanced diet. One is to offer high quality pellets, plus about 20% fruits and vegetables, and the other is to provide a wide variety of nutritious foods. In my opinion, Pionus should not be forced on to a pelleted diet. If, after a reasonable trial, it is obvious that they do not like this food, another kind of pelleted food can be offered or their original diet can be introduced. In theory, processed diets such as pellets and extruded foods are a complete diet. It is recommended that fruits and vegetables are offered up to a certain percentage of the diet. Offering a parrot nothing but pellets would be the equivalent of forcing humans to live on one item of a completely balanced processed food (if such existed). As food is one of the main pleasures in the life of a Pionus parrot (and in humans), this is unacceptable in my view. Unlike chickens, for example, parrots have well developed taste buds and can distinguish even subtle differences in the foods offered. Just like humans, they have their individual preferences.

Most parrots love oil seeds and oily nuts, such as sunflower seed and peanuts, and will eat them to excess, if permitted. Then it becomes hard to persuade them to take a balanced diet. An excess of one seed, such as sunflower, is harmful; sunflower is too high in fats and deficient in calcium and amino acids.

Different parrot species have completely different dietary needs, according to the environment from which they originate. Budgerigars and Cockatiels, from areas that are arid for most of the year, can live on an all-seed diet in captivity. In the wild Cockatiels live mainly on seeding grasses (also on grain crops such as sorghum). Pionus come from localities with a wide variety of fruiting and seeding trees; in the neotropics there is a great diversity in any forested area.

We can look at a list of foods eaten by the two Pionus whose feeding habits are best known in the wild (although relatively unknown, compared with some parrots). According to the *Handbook of the Birds of the World* (volume 4), Blue-headed Pionus feed on the seeds of *Albizia, Anacardium, Caraipa, Dialium, Hevea, Hura, Clusia, Ocotea, Courtoutaria, Inga, Brosimum, Tectona* and *Micropholis*. They eat the fruits of *Tetragastis, Inga, Ficus* and *Euterpe* and the sugary flowers of *Noranthea liana* and of *Erythrina* (coral tree). They also feed on *Goupia, Pseudolmedia, Psidium* (guava), *Mangifera* (mango) and *Pouroma*. Although most of these names mean nothing to the majority of us, this list indicates variety.

In south-eastern Brazil, Mauro Galetti studied the diet of Maximilian's Parrot from August 1988 to December 1999, in a fragmented semi-deciduous forest. It was found to feed on 38 plant species from 18 families. Legumes, including *Erythrina* and *Inga*, comprised 41% of feeding bouts. Seeds made up 70% of the diet, flowers 20%, corn 8% and fruit pulp 2%. The diet changed seasonally. Flower-eating was higher during the dry season. Thirteen species of flowers were eaten; petals and ovary were consumed, also the pollen in at least one species. Maximilian's Parrots, together with two species of monkeys, destroyed the entire flower crop of the coral tree *(Erythrina falcata)*. This suggests that we should be feeding flowers to captive Pionus. However, Galetti points out that the intense flower consumption in that locality might have been due to the fact that the population studied was in a small fragmented forest with lower food resources than continuous forest.

Seeds (especially those of *Inga*) were consumed throughout the year but more often in the wet season (Galetti, 1993). This was just one study. In other localities Pionus are known to feed on figs and on *Araucaria* nuts, for example.

Seed mixtures

If captive birds are fed on a seed-based diet, the mixture should contain no more than 25% sunflower seed. I have found that Pionus readily take the smaller seeds, such as canary and white millet. They also enjoy millet sprays. Most commercial mixtures contain too much sunflower seed. A suitable mixture should contain a good variety of seeds. As an example, in the UK Avian Specific's Parakeet Mixture contains small striped sunflower, buckwheat, paddy rice, white millet, red millet, canary seed, perilla seed, safflower and oats. This is suitable because it is low in high-fat seeds. In the winter, a little hemp can be added for birds kept outdoors in cool climates.

All nuts are too high in fat to offer Pionus on a regular basis, which could result in them becoming overweight unless they take a lot of exercise. I do not recommend peanuts (unless obtained from a health food store), because of the dangers of mould spores inside the shell. Pine nuts can also harbour mould so a sample from any batch should be broken open. An occasional half walnut in the shell can be offered as a treat. Broken walnuts should be obtained only from a health food store as those from other sources could be of poor quality or stale.

Various diets

A typical diet for Pionus was described by German breeder Armin Brockner. The basis was Premium Parrot Mixture by Witte Molen. The maintenance diet, offered from September until January, consisted of 40% Premium, 10% eggfood enriched with vitamins, 5% germinated sunflower seed and 45% fruits and vegetables. The breeding diet, from February until August, consisted of 30% Parrot Dinner (a cooked food) sprinkled with Protamin (Biotropic) and fed twice daily, 10 % germinated sunflower seed, 10% eggfood and 50% fruit and vegetables. The first feed was given at 6am and the second at 6pm (Brockner, 1996).

A comparable diet was fed by David Davenport to his Dusky Pionus. It consisted of Witte Molen parrot mixture, sunflower seed (about 40% of the seed intake), canary seed and millet (20% to 30%), a teaspoonful or two of low-iron eggfood (dandelion and herb) sprinkled on soaked sunflower seed and pulses. The soaked seed was their favourite food and coating it with eggfood ensured that the latter was eaten. Vitamin and mineral supplements were added to the fruit twice weekly. Grapes were their favourite fresh food and these were offered daily. Other fresh foods that were given included orange, apple, banana, pomegranate, kiwi, star fruit, pear, diced carrot, raw beetroot and broccoli (Perry, 1997).

In contrast Terry Needham's Maximilian's did not favour the smaller seeds. Their diet consisted of a parrot mixture that contained about 80% sunflower seed (not ideal) and formed 50% of their intake, plus fruits and vegetables cut into cubes. They would not touch orange. Greenfoods included cabbage and whole dandelion plants. Eggfood was mixed with moist sweetcorn. Cooked chicken was given on occasions. On or off the bone, this is a treat for most of the larger parrots.

Another pair of Maximilian's that refused orange was owned by Peter Yeoman. Their staple diet consisted of parrot mixture, dried tropical fruits, peanuts, millet, apple, sweetcorn, chickweed and toast. When they were rearing young they took CeDe eggfood (offered two or three times daily for the first month), sweetcorn, sunflower seed and toasted brown bread (Anon, 1997b).

Some overseas breeders prefer to feed a blend, or mash, of fruits, vegetables, grains and pulses. In South Africa mashes were or are widely fed to parrots. This is because some breeders ("parrot farmers") have huge numbers of birds and low-cost grains are used in the mash. How appetising this is, is questionable! Dr Deon Smith, who bred the Plum-crowned Pionus there, used a mash consisting of some of the following ingredients:

Cooked rice, maize (yellow and white), maize porridge, wheat, oat porridge and par-boiled sweet potato and pumpkin. This was fed in the afternoon and provided the energy to maintain the birds through the cold nights of the area in which he resided.

In the USA, Alicia McWatters fed organic vegetables, fruits, legumes, grains and seeds to her Maximilian's. The legumes, grains and root vegetables were lightly steamed or par-boiled. In the evening a seed mixture was given. Treats included rice cakes, wholewheat crackers and home-made cornbread (McWatters, 1996).

In the UK, veterinarian Nigel Harcourt-Brown makes up a mixture to feed to his Pionus. It consists of 250g of apple and 200g of carrot chopped into small pieces. To this is added 425g of mixed pulses that have been soaked for 24 hours, then washed well and drained. The pulses used are one part each of mung beans, black-eyed beans, marrowfat peas, chickpeas and a half part of soya beans. This is chopped to a crumbly mixture in a food processor. On this mixture each pair receives about 2ml of Pet Chef Cage and Aviary Bird GP Supplement (vitamins and minerals). This supplement is replaced with Pet Chef Professional Breeder during the breeding season. Pairs in outdoor aviaries also receive a seed mixture; a larger amount of seed is offered during the winter (Harcourt-Brown, personal communication, 1998).

Pulses are often considered to be more palatable when cooked – but they might then be less nutritious. One recipe recommended soaking overnight the following beans: mung, black-eyed, haricot and chickpeas; also maize. These were washed well, just covered with water, then brought to the boil in a saucepan, then simmered for ten to 15 minutes. The cooked beans are then mixed with mixed frozen vegetables (thawed), or with sweet corn; to this is added freshly chopped carrot, celery and green or red pepper, courgettes or green beans. Soaked or sprouted sunflower kernels and a sprinkling of white millet are added to this and, during the breeding season, eggfood and a calcium supplement. This mixture can be varied with dried fruits (raisins, sultanas or figs) that have been soaked for a few hours. As the pulses are a good source of protein, they can also be used as a rearing food.

All cooked and soaked foods should be removed after a few hours (how many hours will depend on the temperature) to prevent bacterial or fungal growth.

Rearing foods

When chicks are in the nest, the parents should be fed at least twice and preferably three times daily. They need a rearing food that contains a good source of protein, ie, one that contains all the essential amino acids. With the exception of sunflower seed, most seeds are low in protein, but the real problem is that the amino acid balance is poor. Certain amino acids are termed essential. If these are present at low levels, other protein components of the food are unavailable for tissue growth. Instead, they will be used as an energy source, thus are of little use to the growing chicks. Nutritionists state that a diet containing 20% crude protein but deficient in certain amino acids would be of no more value than a diet containing 10% very high quality protein. About half the 20 amino acids must be offered to parrots as part of their diet, as they cannot be synthesised in the body.

Among the most important amino acids for growth are proline and glycine, in both of which seeds are deficient. Lysine and methionine are also important for adult birds. Certain supplements manufactured for birds will contain these amino acids. Look at the labels! Good quality protein is essential for normal growth and healthy young. A Pionus chick reaches adult weight at only four weeks on a suitable diet. The importance of an appropriate diet during this period is obvious. However, it is not advisable to suddenly introduce a nutritious food that the parents have never seen before. They might eat it – or they might not. They should already be familiar with the food, even if it is only given occasionally. It is important for breeders to realise that increasing the protein content of the diet at least one month before the breeding season, is an added incentive to go to nest. It also helps to ensure that the female has the necessary nutrients to form eggs, of which protein and calcium are important components.

Pulses

Fruits and vegetables are very low in protein, as are seeds. Sunflower is the exception but this should not form more than about 25% of the diet. Pionus should therefore be introduced to more nutritious foods such as pulses, which are high in protein. The term pulses covers beans and lentils. Suitable types include chickpeas, butter, haricot and mung beans and black-eyed peas. In my experience other beans, such as kidney and pinto, are not favoured. As pulses do not have a high fat content, like sunflower does, they are not as palatable, so the quantity of sunflower seed should be gradually decreased when pulses are fed. Mixing a little sunflower seed with the pulses should encourage the birds to sample them. In the morning, pulses, fruits and vegetables can be fed and, in the afternoon or evening, some seed (including sunflower) should be offered.

Rearing foods

To vary the rearing food, one can make one's own using hard-boiled eggs, carrot, wholegrain bread and a little low-fat cheese. These items are reduced to a fine consistency in a food processor and mixed to a crumbly dry consistency. Too much carrot will make the mixture too moist and unattractive. My experience is that parrots readily take this rearing food and that it is easy to add supplements to it. To make it tempting when first offered, the berries of hawthorn and elder (when in season) and soaked sultanas can be sprinkled on top. As it is time-consuming to make this food, a quantity can be made and stored in a freezer in portions sufficient for one day. Alternatively, one can buy a good quality rearing food such as Parrot CeDe.

Fruits

Pionus will usually eat apple, grapes, pear, orange, banana (not soft or hard). Of the more exotic fruits, pomegranate is their favourite. They also like guavas and cactus fruits. Although soft fruits such as raspberries, gooseberries, plums and peaches can be offered, interest in them might be limited. In late summer and autumn, hawthorn berries are relished for the hard seeds they contain; the flesh is discarded. Elder berries can also be offered to Pionus outdoors. Indoors the juice will stain! Pionus also enjoy eating elderflowers. Tomatoes are excellent for their high vitamin A content, as are apricots, fresh or dried.

Vegetables and greenfoods

All the vegetables mentioned above, as well as peas in the pod, broccoli, spinach beet, courgettes, sweetcorn (frozen) and fresh corn on the cob, cooked beetroot and cooked salad potatoes, can be offered. Raw carrot or probably better still, carrot which has been cooked for five minutes, is a good source of vitamin A.

Blue-headed Pionus at clay lick, Yasuni National Park, eastern Ecuador

Blue-headed Pionus, eastern Brazil
(Pionus menstruus reichenowi)

Blue-headed Pionus
(Pionus m. menstruus)

Coral-billed Pionus – chicks
(Pionus s. corallinus)

Coral-billed Pionus

Coral-billed Pionus

Massena's Parrot *(Pionus t. seniloides)*

Massena's Parrot

Massena's Parrot

White-crowned Pionus – hatching
(Pionus senilis)

White-crowned or White-capped Pionus

White-crowned or White-capped Pionus

Dandelion – the whole plant – is an exceptionally good source and I believe that sowthistle *(Sonchus)* is, too. Most parrot keepers do not make enough effort to collect these wild foods, which are so beneficial and greatly enjoyed. Earth attached to the roots of dandelion or spinach beet, for example, is usually eaten first, perhaps for the minerals it contains. So don't remove it! In July and August seeding dock *(Rumex)* will be enjoyed.

Table foods

Sensible items from the table can make good and enjoyable additions to the diet. These include cooked pasta with a tomato--based source, lean white meat and fish, wholegrain bread, cooked vegetables, pizza and yoghurt.

Vitamin A

The importance of foods or supplements containing Vitamin A has been emphasised. This is because parrots deficient in Vitamin A are highly susceptible to *E. coli* and *Aspergillus* infections, both of which are common in Pionus. *E. coli* is often successfully treated with antibiotics. Sadly, aspergillosis is usually fatal because by the time the problem has been diagnosed (*if* it is diagnosed) the bird has reached the point of no recovery. An easy way to ensure that the diet is not deficient in this vitamin, is to buy a powdered multivitamin supplement made for birds. It will be high in Vitamin A. Cut open a grape (or other favoured food item) with the tip of a sharp knfe and place a little of the powder inside.

Chapter 3

Breeding Pionus

Few Pionus parrots were bred in aviculture until the late 1970s. At that time there was a huge interest in breeding from Australian parakeets and little interest in breeding neotropical parrots which were being imported in large numbers at low prices. In the UK the breeding registers published at irregular intervals by the Parrot Society trace the history of Pionus, when the figures are compared. The registers indicate the number of young reared as reported by members. Not all members participate and not all Pionus breeders belong to the Parrot Society. Nevertheless, these registers are significant in showing trends. The number of Pionus bred is contrasted below with the number of conures which members reported breeding.

Young reported bred by members

Year	1975	1981	1984	1987	1990	1991	1992	1994	1998
Conures	108	112	255	308	481	709	814	1235	1624
Pionus	4	54	14	41	124	149	113	146	216

It should be born in mind that conures are more prolific (and some species lay up to eight eggs) than Pionus. In the late 1980s and early 1990s parrot breeding was at its peak, then there was a drastic decline in the numbers of some of the species that had previously been very popular, such as *Neophemas*. It is therefore interesting to note that when these species were in decline, the numbers of conures and Pionus bred doubled between 1992 and 1998.

Sexing

The plumage of individuals of the same species of Pionus can look quite different. This has led some keepers to believe that they were a true pair. For example, Bryan Peck had two Bronze-winged Pionus. The plumage of one was much brighter and the wing coverts were very bronze. The second bird was much paler. He was convinced that they were a true pair. When he had a number of birds sexed, he decided to include the Bronze-wings. He was shocked to discover that both were females (Peck, 1988).

Now that non-invasive methods of sexing birds using DNA are available, these are highly recommended. They are accurate and no stress is involved, except catching the bird and removing two or three feathers from the breast. Several companies in the UK and in Europe offer this service. They advertise in avicultural magazines. This service is especially useful to breeders who need to make up unrelated pairs. The young can be sexed before they have left the nest.

Laying and rearing

Pionus parrots become noisier and excited when their interest in nesting commences. Copulation is accompanied by distinctive and continuous (but not very loud) vocalisations. There are two methods. In one the male places one foot on the female's back or grasps her primaries, and positions his tail beneath hers. In the other the two birds back up to each other. Mating will occur once or twice daily until the female has laid. Eggs can be expected about three weeks after mating commences. George Smith recorded that two eggs from his *chalcopterus* weighed 22g and 23g; the female weighed 220g (Smith, 1976), therefore her eggs weighed 10% of her body weight. These eggs were unusually large (see table on page 20).

Egg weights and sizes

Species	Egg weight	Egg size in mm (random samples)
menstruus	15g	31 × 25; 32–36 × 24–27
maximiliani	14g, 15g	32 × 24 33.1 × 28.5; 32.6 × 29.0*
corallinus	16g, one at 18g	33 × 23 35.9 × 29.3; 35.3 × 28.5; 35.5 × 28.5; 35.8 × 28.7; 36.0 × 28.8; 37.2 × 28.6*
chalcopterus	14g	29 × 24; 29.5 × 23.3 37.0 × 32.6***
fuscus	12,15–14,6g**	female 1, 34.4 × 27.6; 34.2 × 27.8; 34.2 × 28.2* female 2, 31.4 × 26.9; 31.8 × 28.4; 32.2 × 27.3*
senilis	13g	33.9 × 26.7; 32.8 × 26.7; 32.7 × 26.7; 30.0 × 25.7*
t. tumultuosus	15g	38.3 × 27.4; 34.6 × 27.0*
t. seniloides	16g or more	--------------------

* recorded by Roger Sweeney at Loro Parque
** recorded by John Stoodley
*** recorded by George Smith

The clutch of the larger species consists of three or four eggs. The Dusky and White-crowned might lay five to seven eggs – or even more on occasions. Eggs are usually laid at intervals of three days, or two days; intervals as long as five days are known. The incubation period is about 26 days for each egg and usually commences when the second egg is laid. In a large clutch the incubation period might be longer. For example, Marie Luise Sandkuhler recorded that in a five-egg clutch of Blue-headed Pionus, the first chick hatched after 29 days and the other four after 28 and 27 days (Sandkuhler, 1998a). Incubation is carried out by the female only but some males spend long periods in the nest with the female. The average age of young when they leave the nest is nine weeks, but might be between eight and nine weeks.

Nest inspection can be difficult because the female is very reluctant to move off the nest. The ideal time to inspect is when the female leaves – but this is often easier said than done. The nervous disposition of some wild-caught birds resulted in them killing their young, or mutilating the tip of a chick's beak or toes, possibly due to the stress of nest inspection. Wild-caught Pionus were also liable to desert their young at any unusual disturbance. R. A. Attrill had a cautionary tale to tell: *"I had two pairs of Blue--headed and one pair of Bronzewings with chicks, with clutches of five, three and four respectively. I was well pleased – so much so that I broke the inviolable rule regarding visitors during the breeding season and was proud to show off my success to fellow fancier friends. The result was that all three pairs deserted their young at ten days old (give or take) and when I realised what I had done the clutch of five had two dead and three starving, the clutch of three was intact but on the point of expiry and the Bronzewings had one dead and the remaining three nearly so."* (Attrill, 1991.) One more chick died and the rest were hand-reared and survived.

For nervous birds it is worth installing a nest-box camera – a tiny infra-red video camera. It measures about 10cm (4in) × 5cm (2in) × 2.5cm (1in). These cameras are increasingly being used by parrot breeders. Depending on the size and shape of the nest-box, the camera can be secured either to the outside or laid on the top. It is necessary only to drill a hole in the top of the box, less than 2.5cm wide, as the lens and infra-red sensor are close together. A lead runs from the camera to a monitor or to a television set. Then one can find out exactly what is going on in the nest, and when the female leaves. This is the time, if possible, to close the nest entrance for a couple of minutes and to inspect the young, ring them or change the nesting material. Only handling them will provide sufficient information about their growth and health. It is important to look for signs of rickets – legs, wing bones or spine that are crooked. Calcium supplementation (or injections carried out by a vet before they leave the nest) can result in a cure. Afterwards it is often too late.

At first the male feeds the female and the female feeds the young. After two or three weeks the male also feeds the young. They leave the nest at or before nine weeks. If young are removed for hand-rearing before the age of three weeks, a second clutch will probably be laid.

Chicks can be closed-ringed when aged between 14 and 17 days. Recommended ring sizes are as follows:

P. chalcopterus	8.5mm	UK size T
P. fuscus	8.5mm	T
P. maximiliani	8.5mm	T
P. menstruus	8.5mm	T
P. senilis	7.5mm	S
P. sordidus	8.5mm	T
P. tumultuosus	8.5mm	T

Pionus usually start to breed when aged between three and four years. Some exceptional females might lay when only two years old. The breeder should not expect the first male and female put together to be compatible; like most parrots they are selective about their partners. If two birds do not like each other, breeding attempts will probably fail and one of the pair could be under constant stress. The initial introduction could influence the success or otherwise. It is essential that the birds are introduced in an aviary that neither has inhabited previously. Depending on the circumstances, they might occupy small adjoining cages to get to know each other. If they show a desire to preen each other through the mesh when the cages are placed close together, this is a promising start.

In some species of Pionus, such as *maximiliani* and *tumultuosus*, the head appears speckled with white due to little tufts of white down showing through the contour feathers. However, if over-preening by a bird's mate occurs, the white bases of the head feathers will be exposed – and this is not natural. This sometimes happens in species with a more nervous temperament, such as *chalcopterus*. Severe plucking of the head feathers might occur, which might necessitate separating male and female for a while. If this happens (or if they must be separated for any other reason), the male should be removed from the female's aviary, just in case the male is aggressive towards the female on her return.

Note that serious injury can occur as a result of aggressive encounters. Like macaws, Pionus will often aim at the beak in an agonistic encounter. They must realise that this is a vulnerable area; beak injuries are very painful and can take a long time to heal, so no risks should be taken. Newly introduced birds should be observed via an observation camera and monitor, or observed at a distance from the aviary.

In a compatible pair the breeding season will start with the male trying to feed the female and displaying to her. He raises the feathers on his crown, flares his tail feathers and swaggers about, holding his wings slightly open. An interested female will display in a similar way. This is usually a sign that copulation will follow. The female invites copulation by adopting a stance in which her back is parallel to the perch and her tail is raised.

First recorded breedings in captivity

Species	**Year**	**Breeder**
Blue-headed *(menstruus)*	1890	Maillard, France
White-crowned *(senilis)*	1934	Duke of Bedford, UK
Maximilian's *(maximiliani)*	1970	Beira Zoo, Mozambique
Bronze-wing *(chalcopterus)*	1974	Meli-Park, Belgium
Coral-bill *(s. corallinus)*	1977	Mr & Mrs Stoodley, UK
Plum-crowned *(t. tumultuosus)*	1977	Mr & Mrs Stoodley, UK
Dusky *(fuscus)*	1983	Ramon Noegel, Florida
Massena's *(t. seniloides)*	1986	Karl Diefenbach, Germany

Nest-boxes

The recommended material for nest-box construction is 1.9mm (3/4in) thick marine plywood or a hardwood for outdoor use or 1.25mm (1/2in) for the smaller species housed in a building. The inspection door in the box should be situated just above nest level. It is advisable to place the nest-box where it can be inspected from a service passage, in which case the inspection door will be in the back. If it is necessary to inspect the box from inside the aviary the inspection door should be located at the front or side, so that it is not necessary to take down the box. However, this is not recommended because an "intruder" in the aviary can cause stress to or aggression from the breeding pair.

When constructing the nest-box, note that the entrance should be only just large enough to admit the birds. A perch of hard wood (not dowel, which will be easily destroyed) should be placed below the nest entrance. Strips of wood can be screwed on the inside to allow the birds to climb in and out with ease. A welded mesh "ladder" could be a hazard if a bird became trapped by a nail.

Two sizes are suitable for Pionus. For the smaller Dusky and White-crowned the suggested size is 23cm (9in) square and 41cm (16in) high. Suggested size for the larger species is 25cm (10in) square and 41cm (16in) to 46cm (18in) high. However, the larger Pionus have nested in boxes as large as 31cm (12in) square and 61cm (24in) high, and 25cm (10in) square and 91cm (36cm) high. In hot climates a larger nest-box is suitable. Inverted L-shaped nest-boxes are also suitable, especially if egg-breaking is a problem, because it prevents entering birds from immediately dropping down on to the eggs. A suitable size for the larger Pionus is 55cm (22in) along the top, 46cm (18in) high, with a base 31cm (12in) x 25cm (10in). The jutting out part of the box is 24cm (9in) long and 20cm (8in) high.

Nest-boxes should not be in position throughout the year. Pionus do not normally roost inside. Their sudden introduction in the spring is a stimulus to breeding, especially if a piece of lightweight wood such as pine is tacked over the nest entrance. This makes them determined to enter and the gnawing stimulates breeding behaviour. Another advantage is that they will gnaw this wood away to form an entrance that exactly fits their body size. This lets in less light than a hole that is too large and does not provide a dark enough interior.

Wood shavings are a suitable nesting material. Compressed packs and loose shavings can be obtained from pet shops. The latter might need to be sieved to remove fine particles. The shavings should be packed down in the nest to a depth of 7.5cm to 10cm (3in to 4in). Pieces of rotting (mould-free) tree trunk or small off-cuts of timber can be placed inside the nest. Chewing it up helps to stimulate breeding. Rotting wood should be sun-dried or oven-dried to kill moulds or fungus.

When the young are in the nest it will be necessary to change the wood shavings if they become damp or very dirty, because *Candida* and other fungus could grow. Because Pionus are susceptible to fungal diseases the nest must be kept dry. If the nest remains dry, the shavings might only need to be changed once because the droppings will be reduced to powder. If it is feared that a breeding pair might object to the nesting material being renewed, a little of the old material can be sprinkled on top.

Pionus as foster parents

Most Pionus will hatch eggs and feed chicks of any other Pionus species. This assumes, of course, that they have eggs, or chicks of a similar age. They have also been used as foster parents for Amazons. At Loro Parque, for example, Blue-headed Pionus fed chicks of the endangered Red-browed Amazon *(Amazona rhodocorytha)*. When there is such a large size difference, it would be advisable to remove the chicks for hand-rearing when they were about four weeks old. Proved good parents should be chosen to foster chicks, rather than inexperienced pairs. Pionus can be reared by foster parents of smaller or larger species, provided that they have eggs or young chicks of the same age. At Loro Parque, for example, a White-eared Conure *(Pyrrhura leucotis)* reared a White-crowned Pionus from hatching until the age of two weeks, when it was removed for hand-rearing.

Hand-reared Pionus

If Pionus must be hand-reared from the egg, I would advise the addition of pureed fruit to form at least 10% of the food, whether this is a commercial food or one's own mixture. The ideal fruit is liquidised papaya. In its absence one can use jars or tins of fruit baby food. In my experience, neotropical parrots have a much greater need for some fruit in the food to aid digestion than is the case with most other groups of parrots. Pionus are not the easiest parrots to rear from the egg and can make poor growth gains initially if the diet is not correct. Lack of fruit in the diet might lead to early death because the food is too difficult to digest. If it is preferred, one can make up one's own food. Numerous mixtures have been used. That which I used for five species of Pionus is described under Massena's Parrot.

Chicks are much easier to hand-feed if they have been fed by their parents or by foster parents for a few days. I would not recommend hand-rearing from the egg except by very experienced hand-feeders.

Pionus might be weaned at 14 to 15 weeks but some could take up to 17 weeks. They must be weaned at their own pace, *never* force-weaned.

Initial weight gains are probably higher today now that most people use commercially formulated hand-rearing products.

An example of weight gains, using the home-made mixture described under Massena's Parrot, is given below. The chick was a Coral-billed Pionus that was removed from the nest at 17 days. The weights given are those before and after the first feed of the day. All chicks were spoon-fed.

Age in days	**Weight in grams**
17	84.5 / 92.5
18	90.9 / 95.0
19	94.6 / 98.9
20	99.9 / 107.3
21	104.2 / 111.9
22	107.1 / 115.7
23	111.9 / 119.0
25	118.7 / 126.8
27	129.8 / 138.7
29	137.6 / 148.4
31	154 / 165
33	164 / 177
35	174 / 189
37	186 / 199
39	187 / 204
41	202 / 217
43	213 / 228
45	221 / 236
47	224 / 241
49	235 / 249
61	220 / 237
71	218 / 229

Pionus are often hand-reared to sell as pets – but can hand- -reared birds be used for breeding? As in most parrot species, a lot depends on early socialisation with other members of their own species or genus. If they are kept alone or as pets during the vital few months after independence, males might not be suitable for breeding purposes. They might be too aggressive towards other parrots. If they have always known the companionship of their own species, they appear to be as useful for breeding as parent--reared birds. I participated in a round-table discussion on parent--rearing at the 1996 AFA (American Federation of Aviculture) Convention in California. At this session, chairman Dale Thompson stated that he had third generation hand-reared Pionus that were rearing their own young.

Roger Sweeney (1997b) pointed out the good temperament of young hand-reared Blue-headed Pionus. It makes them ideal cage companions for other young parrots that prove difficult to wean. *"The Pionus can act as 'teacher' birds, being moved between other younger birds which are much slower to wean and encouraging them to eat by themselves. At Loro Parque where many species are constantly being reared, these 'teacher' birds can be extremely useful."*

Chapter 4

Pionus as pets

The species most often kept as pets are Maximilian's and Blue-headed and, in the USA, the White-crowned. In Europe the Maximilian's is the most readily available species. As already mentioned, the smaller size and quieter voices of Pionus, in comparison with many parrots, makes them more suitable for the average home. Hand-reared young obtained at about 14 weeks, or when they are independent, will make wonderful companions – in the right hands. I would recommend a female because mature males can become very excitable and sometimes aggressive when in breeding condition. Females are more gentle and can usually be readily handled by children they know, where as this often is not possible with adult males.

Many Pionus make exceptionally affectionate and docile companions. One advantage is that they are less demanding than many other parrots. But they do love to have their heads rubbed, and will enjoy long periods of this kind of attention. Some hand-reared birds will snuggle up to their owner at this time, especially the more affectionate females. Others will sit quietly while their human companion is watching TV or reading.

Can young parent-reared Pionus make suitable pets? The answer is "yes" in the hands of a patient and sympathetic person. They will take a while to become tame, of course. One of the two most important factors is the age at which the young bird is acquired. This should be at about 15 weeks old, or as soon as it is independent and removed form its parents. Tame pairs (captive-bred rather than wild-caught) will usually produce tame offspring. Young birds copy their parents as regards fear of people or objects. In the UK Peter Yeoman bred from a captive-bred (parent-reared) pair of Maximilian's. When they left the nest their young were so tame and steady that they flew on to his shoulder. Obviously such fearless young would be just as suitable for pets as hand-reared birds.

In my experience, when a Pionus is kept as a pet, it enjoys the company of another Pionus. If the decision is made to buy two, it would be advisable to acquire them at the same time. This would prevent jealousy that can lead to undesirable habits, such as calling for attention. A companion does not prevent two females, for example, from remaining tame with their owner, provided that they were handled daily. However, it would not be advisable to obtain a male and female as when mature they would want to nest and the male would probably (although not invariably) become aggressive towards people.

A young wild-caught White-crowned Pionus in my possession was rather subdued until it was let out of its cage at the same time as my Massena's Parrot. While housed indoors the two became firm friends. The White-crowned would solicit preening by bowing its head and remaining motionless. The two would spend long periods preening each other – but on occasions a complete deadlock was reached. Both birds would remain motionless with bowed heads! The Massena's (a female), always gave in first and began to preen her smaller friend, although she was dominant in other ways. They were, of course, full-winged, yet when given the freedom of the room would spend much time on the top of their cages. They were very quick to learn to go in and out, and proved to be very obedient. In complete contrast to my Amazons, they would return to the cage when told to do so. This is something that they should be trained to do from an early age. They should be praised when they enter the cage and given a tit-bit of a favoured food item. (For further information on the care and training of pet birds, refer to *Why does my Parrot . . .?* Published by Souvenir Press London, also by Rosemary Low.)

Vocalisations

How noisy are Pionus when kept indoors? This will vary according to circumstances but they are quieter than other parrots of comparable size. Ray Dorge keeps a dozen Maximilian's indoors. He noted: *". . . ours like to sleep in, in mid-summer to about 7am, despite our Senegals 6.30am morning shrills, and our Black-headed Caiques rummaging about rattling their toys even earlier than that.*

Our flock of Maximilian's awakens with sporadic, soft guttural chatter. Soon all join in forming a crowd murmur. Then, one or two individuals will raise their voices in call. Others follow suit . . . These calls are not screechy or overly loud, and are quite pleasant to the ear, certainly no louder or harsher than our neighbour's roosters' calls." (Dorge, 2001.)

He further comments that for most of the day the Maximilian's communicate only occasionally through soft-guttural mutterings. Then about 6.30pm all the birds suddenly erupt in "full crow". After about 15 minutes this chorus gradually dies down, and the sounds change to chatter, then silence.

Although many Pionus parrots learn to repeat a few words, they are not renowned for their ability to mimic. The males are more likely to learn to "talk" but some never do so. Some Maximilian's are talkers – but do not expect accurate vocal mimicry, as occurs with a Grey Parrot. The voice is somewhat gravelly! In Canada, Ray Dorge, who has 11 Maximilian's, stated that only one can talk.

Toys and occupation

Pionus kept indoors need regular periods, say twice a day, out of their cage. They need space in which to play on such items as cotton rope hung from the ceiling and branches of trees fixed into a stand, home-made or otherwise. A stand can be an expensive item from a pet store or it could be a coffee table bought in a second hand shop. All one needs to do is drill a hole in the middle of the table and fix in a branch of a tree that is not too hard, such as apple or willow. This will need to be changed regularly. Occupation that keeps a parrot's beak busy is a very important part of keeping it happy. Strips of leather and short lengths of 1.25cm (1/2in) cotton rope, obtained from do-it-yourself stores, can be tied to the cage to provide hours of chewing. Plaited circular cotton swings found in most stores are excellent for the same purpose. The cardboard centres from rolls of paper have a shorter lifespan but provide some amusement. Most Pionus show little interest in the manufactured parrot toys obtainable from pet stores.

Plumage care

A Pionus parrot kept indoors cannot stay in good feather without being sprayed regularly. All that is needed is a plant mister filled with warm water. As soon as it feels the water on its plumage it will open its wings, ruffle its feathers and try to ensure that they all catch the water droplets. Unless the bird is very young, it can be thoroughly wetted; the plumage will become a dark or bronzy colour when wet. Pionus in good health can even be placed outdoors in their cage to catch a rain shower. They should be brought indoors to dry off.

Profile of a companion bird

A letter I received asking for advice contained so many questions of relevance for those who keep a Pionus as a companion that it is worth reproducing here.

"Nearly seven months ago we purchased a male surgically sexed Blue-headed Pionus from our local pet shop. We had observed him for several weeks. He was seven months old, quiet and rather nervous. He had not been handled. At the shop he was housed in an aviary with Budgerigars and Quail and had been fed on seed only.

Less than three months later he became very ill and we took him to an avian vet. An x-ray revealed that our Pionus had heavy metal poisoning. For four days he had intensive treatment. He began to recover but we were told that he might be left with some liver and kidney damage. He eats well but when he must remain in his cage he will not eat much. Then he seems lonely and depressed and we leave the radio on for him. We only go out for about four hours twice a week. The rest of the time he is out of his cage all day. At first he did not want to go in his cage and went on top of the curtain rail each evening and climbed down for about half an hour before agreeing to go into his cage at night. How can we make him go into his cage quickly in an emergency? He will not learn to step up, although we have tried to train him.

We gained his trust and he is a changed bird, no longer nervous and quiet. He spends most of the day out of his cage and climbs around his play gym and our curtains and chats away happily all day. We can now stroke and kiss him and he relishes all this fuss."

I answered as follows:

Your Pionus is lucky to be alive and to have caring owners. He must have had a very bad start in life that left him afraid of people. You have done everything right with the exception of letting him have so many hours of freedom outside his cage. Already you have seen one undesirable result of this: he does not want to eat when confined. By allowing him to live free within the house for most of the time you have inadvertently trained him to regard his cage as a place for sleeping only. This freedom might bring another problem when he is mature. He currently regards the area of the house in which he flies as his territory. When he comes into breeding condition he might "see off" any intruders. This could include one of you – the person to whom he is least bonded.

It is important that you teach him to step up on to your hand on command. You have tried and failed but you have not persevered. All tame parrots can be taught to step up. This is essential. Already you cannot control or catch him. He therefore believes (in fact he is right) that he is in control. He is the flock leader. By training him to respond to your command "Step up!" you will establish the fact that you are in control. If you do not do this you will have more problems with him in time as he exerts his dominance more and more. The reason you failed to teach him might be because you tried to do this in the same room as his cage. In this area he is territorial and more dominant. You should take him to a small room, even the bathroom (with all hazards covered), for training sessions.

If you wish you can use food treats as an incentive to train him to step up and when he goes back into his cage. Withhold his favourite food and offer it as a reward when he responds to training. Even if he only momentarily steps on to your finger or hand, praise him and give him his food treat. He will not be slow to associate doing something right with the appearance of this treat.

Not until he has learned to step up will you be able to alter his eating habits. When you are in control, you will be able to put him away in his cage in seconds. At first you should put him away, then let him out a few minutes later, so that he does not associate being put away with long periods of confinement. Gradually increase the length of time he is in his cage. Only give his favourite food when you put him back or when he goes in on his own. Then he will associate being in his cage with his favourite food. If you eat in the same room as his cage, put him away before you eat but give him something nice (and healthy) from your plate – in his cage. You should very gradually shorten the time he spends out of his cage. He won't like this at first but if you do it gradually he will become used to it.

The final question was this:

"Although he has bonded well with us, we think he needs a playmate. Which parrot species would be suitable? We do not want to lose our special bond with him and we do not want to breed from him."

This is a difficult question to answer. If your son was with his classmates and someone asked you to choose the boy who would make the companion he would enjoy most, you would be highly unlikely to make the same choice as your son. In fact, you would probably not have a clue how to go about it. The only way would be trial and error – but where buying parrots is concerned this is impractical. A friend recently obtained an Orange-winged Amazon to join his other birds: two Greys, an Umbrella Cockatoo, a Green-winged Macaw and a Jardine's Parrot. The Amazon immediately chose one of them as its friend. Who did he chose? The cockatoo! Just as a certain "chemistry" sometimes exists between two people from the moment of meeting, so it does with birds. It is impossible to predict.

Chapter 5

Health care

One of the most important aspects of keeping a Pionus parrot healthy is providing a good diet, as has already been emphasised. Prevention is so much better than cure. But if a Pionus parrot does become sick, early detection will be an important factor in whether or not it recovers. Any departure from normal behaviour, such as eating less or sleeping more, or becoming quieter, should raise the question in the owner's mind: Is my bird sick? A change in the colour or consistency of the droppings without a change of diet, is another indication of ill health.

Many people delay seeking veterinary advice until it is too late. The metabolism of a bird is much faster than that of a cat or a dog, for example. When a bird becomes ill, it deteriorates quickly. If your Pionus stops eating, take him to a vet immediately. He will probably need fluid replacement and could die of dehydration before succumbing to disease. If your bird falls ill or has an accident and you cannot take him to a vet until the next morning, keep him warm. He will lose body heat if he is not eating. The temperature needs to be about 30 deg C (86 deg F).

You can take two precautions in anticipation of your bird being sick. The first is to buy a ceramic infra-red lamp, obtainable from avicultural suppliers and farm supply shops. These are dull emitters. They do not emit red light. They are also virtually indestructible (compared with the glass lamps). The second precaution is to find out the name of an avian vet or a vet who is prepared to handle parrots (not all will do so) as soon as you obtain your first parrot. The third is to have to hand a product for birds that are too sick to eat, such as Poly-Aid (Birdcare Company), a complete diet. This could be administered via a crop tube by a vet.

Aspergillosis

There are several books designed to educate bird owners on health care and disease prevention, one of which should be in the possession of all bird keepers. In this chapter the intention is to discuss problems to which Pionus are susceptible. One of these is aspergillosis. This is a common and usually fatal respiratory disease caused by the fungus *Aspergillus fumigatus*. This fungus is in the air around us but is particularly common on mould – which is why it is so important to keep the cages and aviaries of Pionus clean. Vegetation with mould on it (including compost heaps) close to the aviary) also puts them at risk. Fungal spores might be found in seed that has not been dried properly before storage. Some sunflower seed from each batch should be opened to check for spores; they look like grey or green dust.

Parrots also contract aspergillosis when their immune system is depressed, as a result of disease or stress. Their respiratory systems are very vulnerable to infection when a long-term Vitamin A deficiency occurs. Symptoms include laboured breathing, extreme weight loss and loss of voice. An avian vet can confirm the presence of the disease by anaesthetising the bird and examining it internally with a laparoscope, and with x-rays. Early diagnosis can result in a cure but unfortunately the disease is usually fatal. It is vitally important to consult an avian vet at the first sign of respiratory problems.

Tumours

Pionus, like other neotropical parrots of medium and large size, are also susceptible to tumours, especially as they age. A female Blue-headed Pionus with a very sweet temperament in my care sadly died from a tumour under the wing. Her age was unknown but she was suspected to be quite old. Some cancerous tumours can be treated surgically; others respond to the use of drugs or radiation. A vet can take a biopsy from a tumour to ascertain the type of cancer involved, its treatment and prognosis.

Longevity

Based on our knowledge of other parrots, I feel sure that Pionus have the potential to live to between 30 and 40 years. However, the lifespan of an individual will be dictated primarily by the quality of the diet and attention to maintaining the birds under well-ventilated and dry conditions where fungal infections will not occur. A stress-free environment is also very important for a long and healthy life.

Little has been published regarding longevity in members of this genus. Gail Worth from California, a leading aviculturist there, has no doubts about their potential. She imported Pionus from Ecuador from 1978 to 1980, as adult birds. In 1997 some of them were still breeding (Worth, 1997).

It was not until the late 1970s that there was much interest in breeding these birds so it will be some years before there is useful evidence regarding breeding span and longevity.

Chapter 6

In the wild

Pionus are widely distributed over Central and South America. The main threats they face are loss of habitat and trapping. Unlike most other genera of neotropical parrots, no species is listed as endangered – as yet. This is in contrast to the Amazon parrots. The two main reasons are that none of them are endemic to tiny areas such as Caribbean islands, and because they are not in such demand for the pet trade.

Let us take a quick look at the species from north to south of their range. One of the most numerous is the White-crowned Pionus, found on the Caribbean (eastern) slope of Central America. It ranges from northern Mexico, through Belize, Guatemala, Honduras, Nicaragua and Costa Rica to Panama. The only other species found in Central America is the Blue-headed; it has the most extensive range of any member of the genus. This commences in north-eastern Costa Rica. It is believed that it "invaded" that country only during the 20th century and that its range there is still expanding on the Pacific coast. It continues through Colombia and Ecuador to Peru, Bolivia and Venezuela, through Amazonia to Brazil. The range is not continuous in Brazil where, in the east, the sub-species *reichenowii* is threatened by habitat destruction.

The Coral-billed Parrot also has a discontinuous range, in Venezuela and Colombia. It is found again further south in the Andes of Ecuador, Peru and Bolivia. Also found in this region is the Bronze-winged Pionus, in western Venezuela and in the Andes of Colombia, Ecuador and north-western Peru. The third Andean species is the Plum-crowned Pionus, and its sub-species *seniloides*. The latter occurs from western Venezuela through central Colombia to northern Ecuador and Peru, and the nominate *tumultuosus* is found in the mountains of Peru and Bolivia.

On the eastern side of the continent, the Pionus with the most extensive range is Maximilian's. South of the equator it occurs from northern and central Brazil, through Bolivia, Paraguay and northern Argentina – a very large range from north to south. It is interesting that in some areas of Brazil, such as Espirito Santo, it is sympatric (shares the range) with the Blue-headed Pionus and in Ecuador it is sympatric with the Bronze-winged Pionus in the humid lowlands. The other eastern representative of the genus is the Dusky Pionus, found north and south of the Equator in Venezuela and the Guianas. Another population is found on the distant border of Colombia and Venezuela.

The most successful species are the White-crowned in Central America, the Blue-headed in the north of South America and Maximilian's in the south. By successful, I mean widespread and still numerous and without specialised habitat requirements. It is an interesting fact that "successful" species adapt best to captivity and breed the most prolifically. The widespread Indian Ringneck Parakeet *(Psittacula krameri manillensis)* is a good example. It is certainly true that the three most prolific Pionus species in captivity are the three mentioned here.

Habitat

Pionus are found in a wide variety of habitats from the lowlands up to 3,000m (10,000ft). In the lowlands they occur in forest, cleared areas and on agricultural land. All forest types are used: deciduous and semi-deciduous woodland, seasonally and permanently flooded forest, evergreen forest, pine forest in savannah, palm stands, *Araucaria* forest, coffee and other plantations. The Plum-crowned Pionus can even live in wooded ravines in paramo:

the zone of alpine grasslands above the mountains, and in cloud forest with bamboo thickets. This cloud forest is a fascinating habitat that rivals the Amazon rainforest for biological diversity. Pionus can live almost anywhere where there are trees!

Habits

After the breeding season some species, such as the Blue--headed, Bronze-winged and the Plum-crowned, congregate and move around in flocks in search of food. In contrast, Maximilian's and the Coral-billed are mainly sedentary.

The birdwatcher visiting South or Central America, hoping to see Pionus in the wild, should be aware that they are not easy to observe, except in flight. When feeding they are very quiet and very wary. Centuries of trapping and persecution have made them fearful of man. They are also very difficult to detect once they have landed in a tree. Being familiar with their calls offers the best hope of locating them. The calls of most members of the genus are recognisable as such, except those of the small White-crowned which might be mistaken for an *Aratinga* conure.

Flight pattern

When observing parrots in the wild, it is fascinating to see how flight varies in different genera. Helmut Sick wrote: *"The Pionus have a peculiar way of maintaining themselves in the air with a wing stroke that goes farther below the body than that of any other psittacid. In the forest on a short flight they move without any sound, whereas* Pyrrhura frontalis *loudly rustles its wings going from one branch to another in the same tree."* (Sick, 1993.)

Food

Very few studies have been carried out on the feeding habits of Pionus parrots; there is a great deal to learn. For some species (eg, *sordidus*) there is no specific information. It is known that Pionus feed mainly on seeds, fruits (seeds and pulp), buds and young leaves, flowers (including their nectar) and cultivated crops such as corn. Blue-headed Pionus have been seen feeding on rice crops where they can find a perch to maintain their weight. In *Birds in Brazil*, Helmut Sick noted: "Pionus maximiliani *has been seen gnawing the tips of tall eucalypts until they look decrepit.*"

In Costa Rica, near La Selva, I observed a pair of White-crowned Pionus feeding on the fruits of the pejibaye or peach palm *(Bactris gasipaes)*. This is one of the most common trees of that country, to where it was introduced. These palms, with their spiny trunks, are commonly seen by roadsides and in gardens. They produce large red fruits, the size of a peach, which is relished by the local people when boiled. It is starchy and not sweet.

On one of these palms there was a large hand of ripe fruits; on the previous day it had attracted a pair of White-crowned Pionus and a Chestnut-mandibled Toucan *(Ramphastos swainsonii)*. This morning the Pionus returned to feed on the fruits, which have yellow interiors, but they were soon frightened away by a large fruit-eating bird with a dangerously long bill, a Montezuma Oropendola *(Psarocolius montezuma)*.

I also saw White-crowned Pionus high in the hills above Tui, at 900m (3,000ft), east of Turrialba. Groups of up to about five birds were observed, usually early in the morning, en route to their feeding places. A Pionus food tree in the locality was an *Inga*. A fruiting and flowering specimen attracted a flock of Red-fronted Conures *(Aratinga finschi)*. I watched the conures dextrously removing the black seeds from the pod and also eating the white pulp that surrounds the seeds. I have no doubt the Pionus also used this tree but I was not there long enough to see it.

In Peru, Blue-headed Pionus visit clay licks (barreiros), such as the most famous of all, at Tambopata. At the cliffs macaws and parrots of 15 or more species fly in daily to eat the clay which contains properties believed to detoxify the poisonous seeds they eat. This is one of the most colourful wildlife spectacles on earth, and it is attracting increasing numbers of eco-tourists.

Nesting

Breeding occurs at different times of the year in different parts of the range. In the Blue-headed, for example, it has been recorded in every month of the year in some part of the range. In Panama it takes place from January to May and in the Mato Grosso in June and July, sometimes with a second nest taking it through to November. In Colombia, the Bronze-winged Parrot is said to nest from March to May. The nesting cycle for Pionus takes three months, or longer including nest excavation, where it occurs.

Nest sites are palm trunks (often rotten) and in holes in living and dead trees. The heights of the entrances have been recorded as between 4m and 30m above ground. No doubt many are higher – and inaccessible.

Most parrots are very secretive at or near their nests. Helmut Sick noted: *"A* Pionus maximiliani *may stay for hours at the entrance to the nest, exposing only its head and remaining absolutely immobile while surveying its surroundings . . ."*

Status in the wild

Throughout much of the range of Pionus parrots there has been serious disturbance to and loss of habitat in recent years. Nevertheless, some species are still common in the wild. Up to date information can be found in the *Handbook of the Birds of the World*, volume 4, published at the end of 1997. It is summarised thus:

Blue-headed Pionus: One of the most numerous parrot species in South America. It is common throughout its range.

Maximilian's Parrot: It is common throughout much of its range except in eastern Brazil; locally common in Paraguay and Argentina. It was exported in probably unsustainable numbers from Argentina during the mid 1980s, with 67,815 birds recorded exported from 1981 to 1990. In 1985 more than 25,000 were exported. Despite the ban on bird exports from Argentina in 1986, this species continues to be traded in thousands. (It is considered to be a pest for the damage it does to citrus crops.)

Coral-billed Pionus: It is fairly common throughout most of its range, although forest clearance in Colombia and Venezuela will have caused local declines.

Bronze-winged Pionus: It is declining due to deforestation throughout its range.

White-crowned Pionus: This is a common species, reaching its maximum abundance in Costa Rica. It is possibly now extinct in western Nicaragua due to deforestation. It is naturally rare at the edge of its range in Panama.

Dusky Pionus: It is fairly common throughout its range; decline likely only in southern and eastern parts, due to widespread habitat clearance.

Plum-crowned Pionus: This Pionus is uncommon and local; probable decline throughout most of range.

Massena's Parrot: Also uncommon and local because deforestation has been extensive in the north of its range; habitat destruction is a major threat in Venezuela. It is still common in one area of southern Ecuador. However, this is almost certainly the most threatened of all Pionus.

The species

Quick guide to identification

Species	Head colour	Beak colour
Blue-headed *(menstruus)*	blue with blackish ear coverts	black and pink
Maximilian's *(maximiliani)*	green, black-blue frontal band	dull yellow and grey
Coral-billed *(sordidus)*	green or green and buff with blue on throat	red
Plum-crowned *(t. tumultuosus)*	dark pink suffused with blue-grey	yellow
Massena's *(t. seniloides)*	dark grey, pink, white (intermingled)	yellow
White-crowned *(senilis)*	dull bluish with white crown	dull yellow
Bronze-winged *(chalcopterus)*	dark blue, white on throat	yellow
Dusky *(fuscus)*	bluish-black and buff	black and yellow

All species have red under tail coverts. This colour is tinged with green in some young birds. Note that young of all species might have a red or orange frontal band.

Blue-headed Pionus *(Pionus menstruus)*

Name (menstruus) refers to the red (blood coloured) under tail coverts.

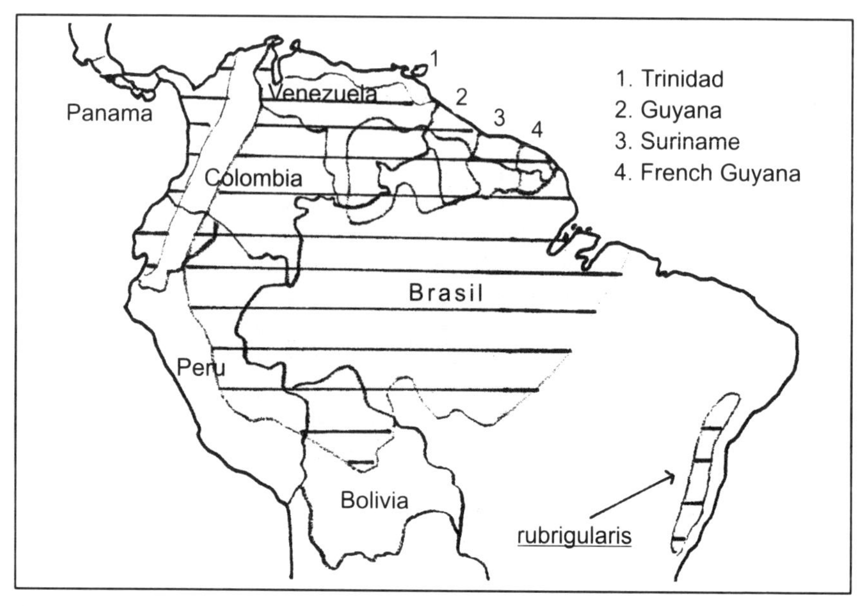

Approximate range of the Blue-headed Pionus *(Pionus menstruus)*

DISTINGUISHING FEATURES: A beautiful bird with the intense blue of the head contrasting with the green body. The hint of pink on the throat is repeated on the upper mandible, which is otherwise black.

Length: 28cm (11in).

Weight: 230g, average of 11 birds; range 206 g to 270g (Harcourt--Brown, pers. comm., 1998).

IMMATURE PLUMAGE is variable.

- There is a less extensive area of blue on the head, with some green suffusion.
- The body plumage might be as colourful as that of an adult, or even more so.
- Some birds lack the black ear coverts.

- Many have a pinkish or orange frontal band that disappears after a few months or might be present for up to one year. It takes two years or more for the full depth of blue of the head colour to be acquired.
- Newly fledged young have both mandibles pale, with part of the upper mandible dark.

SUB-SPECIES: *P. m. rubrigularis* has a more conspicuous area of pink on the throat but the shade of blue is duller. There is a rare sub-species, *P. m. reichenowi*, in which the underparts are light blue; this area is suffused with green in young birds. The pink bases to the feathers of the throat are absent. The under tail coverts are margined with blue – in contrast to those of the other sub-species which are margined with green in young birds. The beak is lighter; the mandibles are yellowish, tinged with grey. This Brazilian sub-species is probably non-existent in aviculture outside Brazil.

COLOUR VARIATION: Roger Neckles, a well-known bird photographer, told me that in Trinidad he saw a small flock of this species in which all the young had pink hoods. This is in contrast to the usual immature plumage of *menstruus* in Trinidad in which the young normally have pink on the forehead and cheeks.

AVICULTURE: The Blue-headed Pionus is probably the most sought-after species of Pionus as a pet and, of the generally available species, as an aviary bird. Its contrasting colours and the depth of blue produce an extremely beautiful bird. As a pet it is renowned for its gentle temperament. Females are especially sweet-natured.

This Pionus used to be the most frequently bred species in Europe, partly because it was imported in greater numbers than any other. Numerically, Maximilian's is now the stronger species and is bred more frequently. The clutch size is four or five. Newly hatched young have long white down on the upperparts. Marie Luise Sandkuhler recorded the weights of five newly hatched chicks in one clutch as 9g, 11 g, 10g, 12g and 10g (Sandkuhler,

1998a). These chicks were well fed and the parents could be heard feeding them during the night. After the fifth week the chicks were fed by the male, and the female spent long periods outside the nest. From the sixth week the young would be removed from the nest for a while, every second or third day, to accustom them to people. Just prior to fledging they weighed between 240g and 260g; afterwards they weighed about 215g. When they fledged in the ninth week they were not shy. At 12 weeks old they were independent.

In the following January the female laid five more fertile eggs. Three chicks hatched. They were ringed between 18 and 20 days with 9 mm rings. They then weighed between 160g and 180g. In June the female laid four eggs which produced four more young. All 13 had a red or yellow-red frontal band in nest feather.

Also in Germany, Armin Brockner kept his pair in an inside aviary measuring 2.5m (7ft 6in) long, 91cm (3ft) wide and 2m (6ft) high. In his opinion, that was the absolute minimum size for a pair. He would have preferred them to have access to an outdoor flight, where they could rain-bathe. Four weeks after copulation was first observed the female laid three eggs at intervals of three days. The first chick hatched after 26 days. It was covered with long white down. Three days later the second chick hatched. The third egg was infertile (Brockner, 1996).

COUNTRIES OF ORIGIN: Central America and South America. *P. m. rubrigularis* is found from northern Costa Rica, through Panama to Colombia and western Ecuador. The nominate race occurs in eastern Colombia, eastern Ecuador, eastern Peru and northern Bolivia, through Brazil and in the Guianas and Trinidad. *P. m. reichenowi* is found in eastern Brazil.

Habitat: It is found up to 1,400m (4,600ft) in woodland, including seasonally flooded forest, plantations and semi-open areas, also in stands of *Mauritia* palms. In Trinidad it is found at higher elevations than the common Orange-winged Amazon *(Amazona amazonica).*

Status: CITES Appendix II. Common in most parts of its range.

Maximilian's Parrot *(Pionus maximiliani)*

Maximilian's Parrot

Maximilian's Parrot

Coral-billed Pionus, Mindo
(Pionus sordidus mindoensis)

Sordid Parrot *(Pionus s. sordidus)*

Plum-crowned Pionus
(Pionus t. tumultuosus)

Recently weaned Blue-headed Pionus

Dusky Pionus *(Pionus fuscus)*

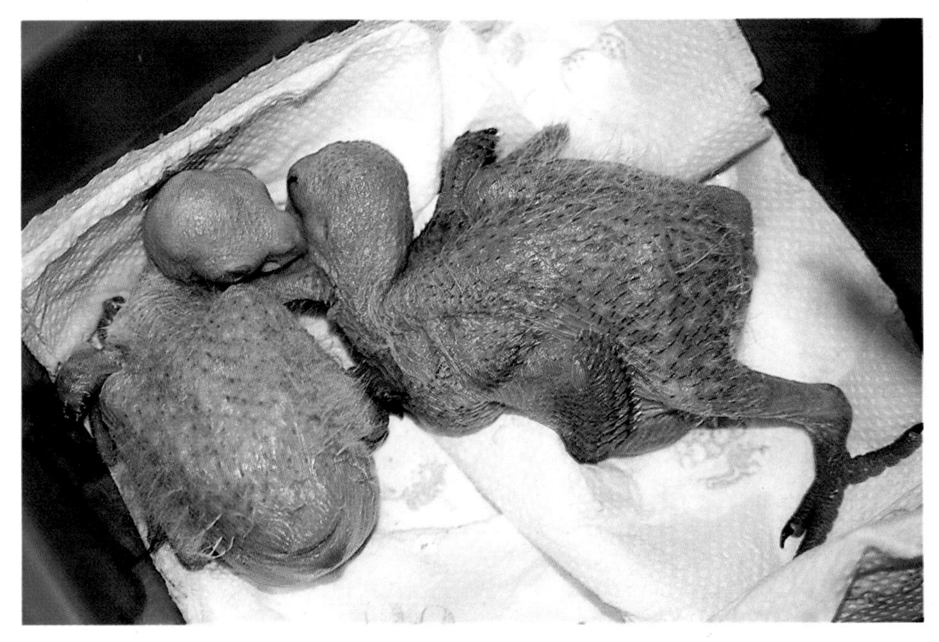

Dusky Pionus

Dusky Pionus

Bronze-winged Pionus *(Pionus chalcopterus)*

Soaked peas, beans and grains suitable for Pionus

Maximilian's Parrot *(Pionus maximiliani)*

Scaly-headed Parrot

Named after Maximilian Alexander Philip Prince zu Wied--Neuwied (1782–1867). He was a German explorer and collector in Brazil.

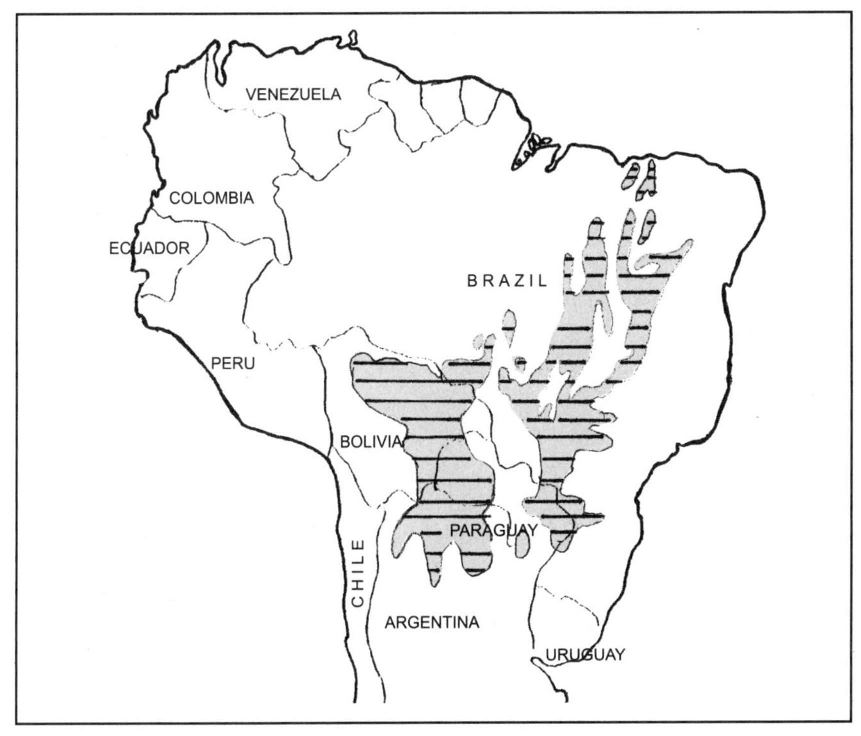

Approximate range of the Maximilian's Parrot *(Pionus maximiliani)*

DISTINGUISHING FEATURES: green with bronze, with dull mauve or blue on the throat. The head usually looks speckled with white. The bronze upper wing coverts are a beautiful feature of some birds.

Length: 29cm (11in).

Weight: 230g, average of 20 birds; range 200g to 240g (Harcourt--Brown, pers. comm., 1998).

IMMATURE BIRDS: The plumage is duller. Most birds have a band of red on the forehead, or red flecks.

SUB-SPECIES: Four races have been described but they might not be easy for the aviculturist to recognise. Also, there might be intergrades in the wild between *melanoblepharus* and *siy*, and *siy* and *lacerus*. Note that the nominate race is almost unknown in aviculture. Overall the plumage is lighter green. In *melanoblepharus* the back and underparts are darker green and the chin and throat are darker blue. In *siy* the overall shade of green is paler, more bronze. Chin and throat are reddish-purple; some feathers are tipped with blue. It is described as differing from *siy* in its slightly larger size and in the more extensive and deeper blue on the throat.

The prominent area of bare skin surrounding the eye is mainly white; in *lacerus* it is transformed into half circles by touches of dark grey in some birds, including the nominate race. In *melanoblepharus* the orbital skin is dark. In all sub-species the beak is dark grey and yellow.

AVICULTURE: Maximilian's is a good subject for the newcomer with Pionus. It nests readily and will often be double-brooded, if eggs or young chicks are removed. There is a good demand for the young, as prices are reasonable. Someone who knows a lot about the pet potential of this species is Eb Cravens from Hawaii. When he lived in the USA he owned a pet shop and sold Blue-headed and Maximilian's. He wrote: "*. . . in all the years of selling these psittacines, we never had a dissatisfied owner come in to exchange or return a Pionus. Some were rowdier than expected (especially young males); some made more noise than anticipated (again the boys!); but all were welcome in the home in the long-term. And for the conscientious bird shop trying to place its baby birds as well as to retail them, this permanence with Maxis and the other members of the genus was a real bonus. Yes, Pionus parrots are excellent choices for those who do not wish their new pet to dominate their busy lives.*"

"Bathtime, too, is a treat with a Maxi. These guys love the water – spray bottles preferred, with any greenery thrown in for realism, please!

When bathing a Maximilian's, it is essential to wet them very well all over or they will not be satiated, then be sure to give them a warm dry place to preen and dry off . . .

Our Maxis were always well behaved, solitary parrots who seldom screamed, rarely chewed on things, gave moderate attention to toys and never picked fights. We have heard of aggressive males in puberty and of screechers declaring their territory in morning and evening, but as babies, this was never seen. Lovers of the more boisterous and rowdy psittacines may imply that pionus parrots are somewhat 'boring'. Yet I find that species of birds who know how to keep themselves occupied and are not always demanding touch or activity with their owner are a joy to keep, especially in a home with more than one pet parrot. Well socialised Maxis are all this and more." (Cravens, 1997.)

In Sweden, a pair of *siy* in the care of Mats Tell reared young in 1980. They were housed in a 2.1m (7ft) aviary within a birdroom with a 3.6m (12ft) outdoor flight. This was south-facing, with one quarter of the roof covered in fibreglass and with gravel on the floor. Towards the end of April, the female laid four eggs. Three hatched, the first on May 22. The first young one left the nest on July 14, followed by the other two five days later (about 54 days in the nest). All three had red frontal bands; although they did not moult, by the end of the year this colour had disappeared, and these feathers were blackish. Their first complete moult commenced in July of the following year. In 1981 the female laid five eggs. The first chick hatched on May 17. It left the nest on July 11, followed by three more on July 16,18 and 24. These young had blackish frontal bands (Tell, 1983).

Ray Dorge wrote about a pair of Maximilian's that breed in his house (in Canada) and are allowed out of their cage. The female does not start to incubate until the second egg has been laid but she will sometimes play on the "play-gym" after the first egg is laid. After the second egg she rarely emerges from the box during the incubation period. It is of interest that after the chicks are two weeks old, she roosts outside the nest-box entrance. She always lays five eggs.

When the youngest chick is three weeks old, all the chicks are removed for hand- rearing. The parents are then removed from their breeding cage to the usual cage. They stay there, with the opportunity to exercise on the playgym "to get themselves back into prime physical condition". Ray Dorge states: *"They are gentle, highly intelligent, undemanding, quiet and relatively easy to breed."* (Dorge 1996.)

COUNTRIES OF ORIGIN: South America – widespread. The nominate race is from north-eastern and central-eastern Brazil. From central Brazil, eastern Paraguay and north-eastern Argentina comes *melanoblepharus*. The sub-species *siy* comes from the Mato Grosso region of Brazil, eastern and central Bolivia and much of Paraguay. In the north-west region of Argentina *lacerus* is found.

Habitat: Forest and open scrub woodland. In the north and west of its range it prefers deciduous and gallery forest such as *caatinga* and Chaco. *Caatinga* is the sub-arid region of north-eastern Brazil with succulents, cacti and trees (often spiny) which are leafless for months; in the short rainy season the region becomes green and flowery.; In the south-east of its range, *maximiliani* favours more humid habitats, including *Araucaria* forest (Collar in del Hoyo, Elliott & Sargatal, 1997).

Status: CITES Appendix II. It is common except in northern extremities of its range.

Coral-billed Pionus *(Pionus sordidus)*

Red-billed Parrot

Meaning of *sordidus*: dirty, shabby. (The Pionus must surely be the most unfairly and inaccurately named group of parrots in existence!)

Approximate range of the Coral-billed Pionus *(Pionus sordidus)*

DISTINGUISHING FEATURES: The variation among the subspecies is great (see page 54); however, the red bill is the feature which distinguishes it from other Pionus.

Length: 28cm (11in).

Weight: 240g to 270g.

SUB-SPECIES: The nominate race looks totally different to *corallinus*; it is much lighter – pale olive green. The head is green, with the feathers of the crown and nape broadly edged with dark blue; the feathers of the cheeks are olive, margined with dark blue. The feathers of the throat and upper breast are blue, tinged with green. On the breast and abdomen the feathers are dull olive, margined with buff. On the back the feathers are dull olive with lighter margins and tinged with blue.

P. s. corallinus is larger and greener than the other races, with the upperparts tinged with grey and blue. *P. s. antelius* is paler than the nominate race with less blue on the throat and upper breast. *P. s. saturatus* is overall dull and dark; *ponsi* is even darker. According to the photograph in Thomas Arndt's *Lexicon of Parrots* (page 307), it is distinctively coloured with broad buff margins to the khaki feathers of the underparts. There is a little grey-blue at the throat. *P. s. mindoensis* is lighter throughout and more bronzy with narrower blue margins to the head feathers.

Armin Brockner from Germany sent me a photograph of *Pionus sordidus mindoensis* that he photographed in Ecuador. Its colouring was paler throughout. The centres of some of the wing coverts were grey but the margins were very faint – not dark. The blue area on the throat and upper breast was present. The rest of the underparts were a delicate shade of buff-pink, becoming olive--buff on the lower abdomen.

In *sordidus*, identification is not easy; refer to photographs of all sub-species in the *Lexicon of Parrots*. Note, however that some of the birds depicted are immature.

IMMATURE PLUMAGE differs from that of adults in

- Duller head coloration but most birds have a touch of pink on the forehead.
- Under tail coverts are said to be yellow-green marked with red, but they were red in the young I have seen of the nominate race and of *corallinus*.

- Some newly fledged young are very colourful – but the colours soon fade. Some bred by John Stoodley (sub-species not stated but almost certainly *corallinus*), had "blue, pink, golden-green and almost gold on the breast and about the head, but the brilliance of the colours seemed to fade, as did the facial red soon after the birds were separated from their parents". (Stoodley, 1978.)
- Captive-bred young from a pair of the nominate race were fairly close to *maximiliani* in appearance, except for the orange bill.

AVICULTURE: Except for a short period in the 1970s, this species has always been rare in aviculture. After export ceased in the early 1980s it quickly became rare again. It was never exported in large numbers, probably because trappers perceived it as being a relatively dull coloured parrot. The sub-species available then was *corallinus*. I have seen another sub-species in captivity on only one occasion. This was the nominate race in a private collection.

When I had all species of Pionus in my care at Loro Parque, this was one of my favourites. I have fond memories of the two breeding pairs of the nominate race. They were wonderful parents. One female reared a very precious chick along with her own, a Massena's Pionus, until I removed it to hand-rear. In her next nest she reared a White-crowned Pionus with her own.

One of these females was the subject of my most embarrassing memory from my days at Loro Parque. The pairs were kept in the original off-exhibit breeding centre. The nest-boxes were in a rather cramped, unprotected area behind the aviaries. One day when I was inspecting the nest-box the female suddenly leapt at my hand. As I withdrew it, she came out attached to it and flew off into the park. It all happened in an instant! I was shocked. There was no sign of her and I was very upset. However, several weeks later she miraculously reappeared. I had no idea where she had been as she had not been seen in the park, an oasis in quite a built-up area. She was caught and re-united with her mate. No doubt she had quite a story to tell him – and I was vindicated!

I remember how beautiful the chicks were. They had dense white down on crown, nape and upperparts, which was still visible when the contour feathers were erupting. The beak colour starts to change from whitish to pale coral when the chick is about three to four weeks old.

COUNTRIES OF ORIGIN: South America. The nominate race comes from northern Venezuela. From north-eastern Venezuela comes *antelius; ponsi* the darkest race originates from north-western Venezuela, west to the foothills of the Santa Marta Mountains. *P. s. corallinus* comes from the eastern Andes, from Colombia, southwards through Ecuador and eastern Peru to northern Bolivia; *P. s. mindoensis* is found in western Ecuador.

Habitat: Lowland and montane forest, also cloud forest from 100m to 2,400m (330ft to 7,900ft), but usually at 500m to 1,500m (1,600ft to 4,800ft). This species also occurs in secondary growth and in plantations.

Status: CITES Appendix II. Fairly common.

Plum-crowned Pionus

(Pionus t. tumultuosus) **Speckle-faced Parrot**

Meaning of *tumultuosus*: restless, disorderly; the reasoning is not clear, especially when it would have been more logical to refer to its most distinctive and beautiful feature – its head colour.

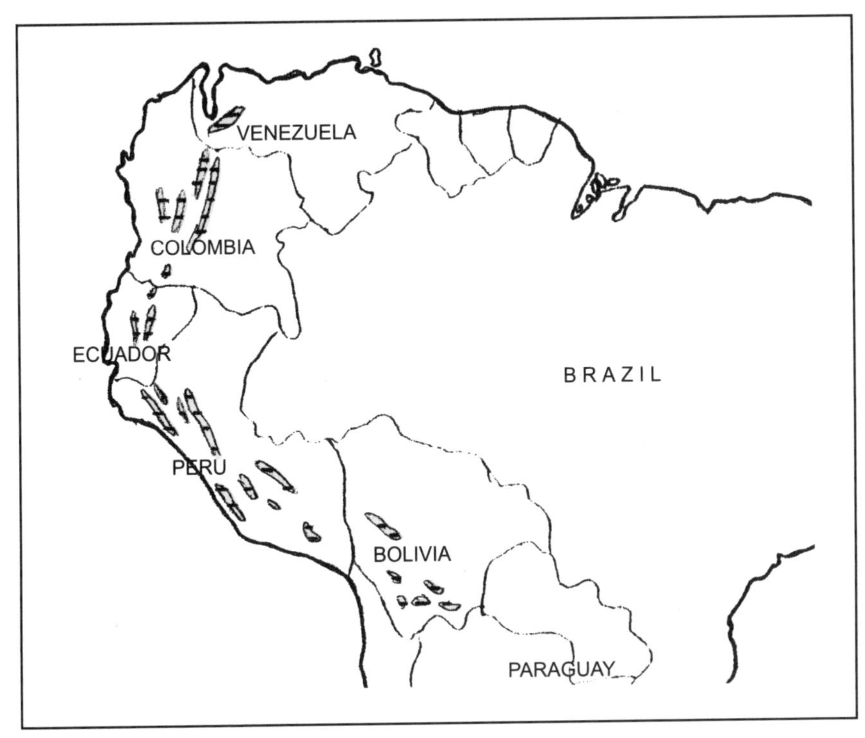

Approximate range of the Plum-crowned Pionus *(Pionus t. tumultuosus)*

DISTINGUISHING FEATURES: The head is dark rose or light plum-coloured; the plum colour spills down on to the throat, the feathers of which might be marked with bluish-grey – the colour of the upper breast and the ear coverts. The head is marked with little tufts of white down and the feathers of the lores and those beneath the eyes have white or pink centres.

Length: 11cm (29in). Weight: about 240g.

I previously described the Plum-crowned Pionus as follows: *"This is a very beautiful bird with unique head coloration which is variable, being intense rich plum on the crown and forehead in adult males in breeding condition and duller in other birds. The centre of each feather is white, but this can be seen only when the feathers are parted. The nape is blackish-green, the rest of the upper parts being dark green . . ."* (Low, 1992.) The underparts are mainly green; the tail is green marked with red at the base and blue on the outer feathers.

SUB-SPECIES: *seniloides*. See page 60.

IMMATURE PLUMAGE is variable. One that was partly hand-reared at Loro Parque was as colourful as the adults (Sweeney, verbal communication, 1998). Others are less colourful; the head and breast are mainly green and the throat is pink. Under tail coverts are yellowish-green, marked with pink at the base.

AVICULTURE: This is often considered to be the most beautiful member of the genus. In aviculture it has always been extremely rare and expensive. In 1974 the Plum-crowned Pionus was imported into Europe for the first time. A few more came in during the mid-1970s. I suspect that the survival rate was low. It seems that like other parrots from the high Andes, some do not easily adjust to life at a low altitude.

The first breeders were John and Pat Stoodley, in 1977, from one of three pairs imported in 1974. In Germany, Karl Diefenbach also bred this species, as did Dr Deon Smith in South Africa. Unfortunately, all these successes were short-lived and the Plum-crowned Pionus has almost died out in aviculture. This is especially sad when one considers that in 1983 John Stoodley recorded that he had bred this species since 1977. That year alone 12 were reared. The total must have been considerable and I believe that most of the young were exported.

The first breeding success at Loro Parque occurred in 1997 from the female bred by Dr Smith in 1992. I recall receiving some worried telephone calls from Dr Smith when his pair produced chicks. He had a number of problems. The extremes of climate where he lived in South Africa were not conducive to breeding this Pionus. He could not maintain the birds for long, in spite of constructing climate-controlled aviaries for them.

Nevertheless, a female survived to pass on her genes, when paired with the male who had been on his own at Loro Parque when I was there ten years earlier. In 1994 the pair had been moved to the new Pionus aviaries on exhibition in the park. (The area was previously an enormous lily-bed, free of aviaries.) Each aviary is surrounded by planting, in one of the more secluded corners of the park. In 1997 the female laid three eggs in February. Her incubation was somewhat erratic, thus the eggs were moved to an incubator. The embryos began to develop but did not survive past 16 days.

The female laid a second clutch, starting at the end of April. Two of the four eggs were transferred to an incubating female Maximilian's; two remained with the Plum-crowned. The latter eggs did not hatch but the Maximilian's hatched both the Plum--crowned's eggs. When the chicks were handled to ascertain if they could be ringed, crop and cloacal swabs were taken. The chicks appeared to be in good condition but the cultures produced a significant growth of *E. coli.* A three-day course of antibiotics was administered. The wood shavings were changed regularly to reduce the possibility of fungal infection. But one of the chicks died in the nest; the autopsy was inconclusive. The surviving chick was removed to the clinic. After two days it was introduced to a young Lilacine Amazon *(Amazona autumnalis lilacina)*, whose companionship gave it more confidence. After one week it started to eat on its own. Meanwhile, the Plum-crowned had reared a Maximilian's from a fostered egg (Sweeney, 1997a).

COUNTRIES OF ORIGIN: Peru and Bolivia. It is found in the Andes in south and central Peru and in the La Paz and Cochabamba departments of Bolivia.

Habitat: Sub-tropical forests and cloud forest with bamboo thickets, as high as 3,000m (1,000ft).

Status: CITES Appendix II. Uncommon and local; almost certainly declining.

Massena's Parrot *(Pionus tumultuosus seniloides)*

Grey-headed Parrot, White-headed Parrot

Meaning of *seniloides*: resembling the aged (a reference to the white-flecked head).

TAXONOMIC NOTE: *P. t. seniloides* was considered to be a separate species by taxonomists until the mid-1970s. Then two renowned ornithologists, John P. O'Neill and the late Theodore Parker, discovered that the range of the two forms is almost continuous. They stated:

"After careful scrutiny of the specimens available to us we have come to the conclusion that the only difference between P. seniloides *and* P. tumultuosus *is the amount of rose or plum color present in the plumage of the head and belly. The northern birds,* P. seniloides, *have the head strongly marked with this color and have solid green bellies. The older birds of either form apparently have the greatest saturation of the rosy coloration in their plumage . . ."* (O'Neill and Parker, 1977.)

DISTINGUISHING FEATURES: Similar to the nominate race but lacking the plum colour on the head. Some birds have the underparts wine coloured; in other birds they are partly green. There is some variation in the areas of vinous or dark mauvish--blue; in some birds this extends to the red of the under tail coverts.

Length: 28cm (11in).

Weight: 229g (one only: a female collected in Peru).

IMMATURE BIRDS differ from adults in having:

- The underparts green.
- Some have pink feathers on the forehead.

They could almost be mistaken for Maximilian's at this stage, except that the wings are a uniform green.

AVICULTURE: It is ironic that the first Pionus I ever kept was one of this sub-species – the rarest Pionus in aviculture. Yes, "Pinkie" introduced me to this genus. Anyone who has kept birds throughout his or her life will have fond memories of a few outstanding individuals. One such is the Massena's Parrot that I found in 1969 on a trade stand at the National Exhibition of Cage & Aviary Birds. At this time there was no interest in Pionus. I bought her for 13 pounds! I recorded:

"It was fairly young, although not tame, when obtained, but allowed me to rub its head. It took a year for it to become completely confident: one day, after weeks of hesitation, it landed on my shoulder when let out of its cage. After that it climbed over me every day without a moment's hesitation . . .

The Massena's is such an engaging little parrot that its misdemeanours (which include eating the spines of my three volumes of Greene's Parrots *– a rather expensive meal) are easy to overlook. It is not the mismarked monstrosity that the late Duke of Bedford would have one believe. His description of 'the untidy looking Pionus seniloides which has the appearance of a bird making a half-hearted effort at albinism or suffering from weak feather growth' was entirely unjustified."* (Low, 1972.)

It was also inaccurate. Some birds are very beautiful. On page 329 of volume 3 (Mittel- und Sudamerika) of Franz Robiller's *Papageien* is a photograph of an extremely colourful pair that was at Vogelpark Walsrode in Germany.

"Pinkie", as my Massena's was called, typified the qualities for which Pionus are sought as pets – sweet and gentle. She gave me so much enjoyment. I never expected to find her a mate. Perhaps if I had not done so she would still be with me. After several years I located a male – in Scotland. It was the third bird of her kind of which I knew in the UK. He was not at all tame and he was exceedingly nervous. He seemed ill at ease in captivity. The two birds were placed in an outdoor aviary and appeared to be compatible. Alas, early one morning he killed the female. Finding her was one of the worst moments of my lifetime in aviculture . . .

It was more than a decade before I had Massena's Parrots in my care again. When I joined Loro Parque as curator in 1987, there was a pair in the collection. That year the female laid two eggs. One chick hatched but was unfortunately buried in the nest litter soon after. The first egg had been laid on the floor. In 1988 the pair nested early. Again the first egg was deposited on the floor. Five more eggs were laid; the high number was due to their immediate removal. One egg was quite badly damaged and was patched with porous tape soon after the damage occurred. The chick hatched but sadly died at day one, probably due to dehydration. Three other eggs in an incubator failed to develop or were infertile.

On January 31 a new-laid egg from the *seniloides* was placed in the nest of a trusted female Coral-billed who had eggs. It had hatched by February 26. After drying out, the newly hatched Massena's was covered in white down that was long on the head and back. The chick was fed by the Coral-bills until the age of eight days when I removed it for hand-rearing. At the same time I removed one of the Coral-billed chicks.

By March 16 (19 days) the Massena's eyes were open – but not fully. The long down had diminished but small tufts of down were then apparent on the cheeks and underparts. The skin looked greyish with the many feathers developing below it. By April 8 the wing coverts had erupted but the primaries were only just starting to erupt. The head was covered in erupting feathers and much white down. On the body the down was dense and white. By April 17 the totally green wings and head seemed to emerge from a mass of white down.

By April 30 the young Massena's was fully feathered except for the shorter tail. Its growth had been less rapid than that of the Coral-bill because it digested food more slowly. The food had contained about 10% liquidised papaya – the best aid to digestion I know. The rearing food consisted of baby cereal, wheat germ cereal, a little peanut butter and, liquidised with water, papaya, carrot and apple, plus a calcium and mineral supplement.

The weight of the Massena's did not equal that of the Coral-bill (which was one week older) until the weaning stage. May 3 was the first day on which the Massena's weighed more than the Coral-bill. Both were weaned by the time they left the hand--rearing room at 15 weeks (Low, 1988). This Massena's was still at Loro Parque, on exhibit, more than a decade later. There were then two pairs in the collection. This was the only breeding to be recorded there and one of only two of which I am aware.

The first had occurred in Germany two years previously, in 1986. A pair belonging to Karl Diefenbach had three eggs, two of which hatched. This Pionus remains extremely rare in aviculture. Apart from those at Loro Parque, I did not encounter it again until 1997. I was surprised to see eight birds in the Fundacion Ara collection in Mexico. They were kept in a colony (to allow them to choose their own mates) in a large aviary that measured 7m × 5m wide × 4m (23ft ×16ft × 13ft). No bonding had occured at the time, although they had entered the nest-boxes.

COUNTRIES OF ORIGIN: Venezuela, Colombia, Ecuador and Peru. It is found from north-west Venezuela, through western Colombia (central and eastern Andes), to both slopes of the Andes in western Ecuador and northern Peru.

Habitat: A mountain species, it occurs in humid forested areas above 1,800m (5,900ft) in the upper sub-tropical zone and might be found as high as 3,000m (9,800ft).

Status: CITES Appendix II. Uncommon and local. It has declined throughout its range, especially in Venezuela, as a result of habitat destruction.

Bronze-winged Pionus

(Pionus chalcopterus)

Meaning of *chalcopterus*: metallic-winged.

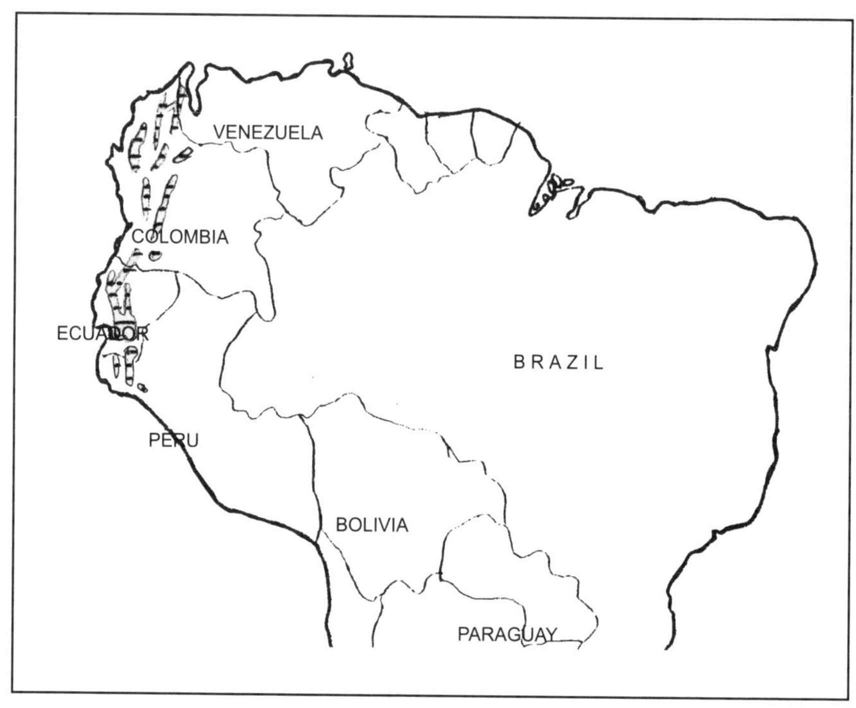

Approximate range of the Bronze-winged Pionus *(Pionus chalcopterus)*

DISTINGUISHING FEATURES: It has a remarkable combination of colours, being mainly dark blue with pink on the throat, bronze wings and bright skyblue under wing coverts. The scarlet under tail coverts, shiny blue underside of the tail and dark bronzy-blue and deep blue plumage above complete this unique colour scheme.

Length: 28cm (11in).

Weight: 210g, average weight of nine; weight range 194g to 228g (Harcourt-Brown, pers. comm., 1998).

IMMATURE PLUMAGE differs from that of adults in having:
- The wing feathers edged with green – or they might have bronze wings.
- The feathers of the underparts brown, tinged with blue and edged with green.
- The skin surrounding the eye yellowish.

SUB-SPECIES: *cyanescens* is doubtfully distinct. It is said to be purer blue on the underparts; slightly smaller size.

MUTATION: In the early 1980s a mutation Pionus, a wild-caught bird, was imported into the UK. It was obtained by Raymond Sawyer. A dilute mutation, it was mainly pale yellow in appearance with a yellow beak and dark eyes. I believe that it was *chalcopterus* because of the extensive pink markings on the upper breast, the yellow-bronze appearance of the wings and the red markings in the tail. It was kept with a *chalcopterus* but breeding did not occur.

AVICULTURE: This Pionus has the advantage of not normally making any loud or harsh calls; its vocalisations consist mainly of a strange rasping sound. Its disadvantage is its nervous temperament. In *Parrots, their care and breeding* I wrote of wild-caught birds (obtained in the 1970s):

"... it is a highly nervous species, becoming subject to stress in conditions under which an Amazon, for example, would not bat an eyelid. One night, in January 1978, there was a noisy storm with high, whining winds; next morning a female Bronze- wing, which had been in my possession over seven years was found dead on the floor, although the aviary was a sheltered one in an open-fronted brick building. Autopsy revealed that the bird was in perfect condition."

I also noted of this species: *"... perhaps due to the stress of captivity, mated pairs tend to overpreen each other's heads; for this reason, on one occasion I had to separate my pair during the winter months to allow the regrowth of the head feathers. One bird then removed the feathers from its back and thighs. For a couple of years, the head of the other bird was completely bare, giving an unfortunate vulturine appearance. However, the feathers did grow when the birds were separated. One January I had to separate the pair when the male attacked the hen's head; the pair was reunited after five or six weeks and then nested."*

My pair was the first in the UK for which a successful parent-rearing was recorded – in 1976. Because the female was so nervous and secretive, never leaving the nest when anyone was in the vicinity, nest inspection did not take place. Her first egg was laid about May 18. On June 17 the peculiar quavering cry of a chick was heard. The female was not seen in the aviary until more than four weeks later. I had not seen her for two months, until the middle of the rearing period, when she would occasionally look out of the nest entrance. The male would feed her from the nest-box perch. On July 28 she was sitting unconcernedly in the aviary, for the first time. Thereafter she spent increasing periods in the flight. At 7pm on August 18 a young Bronze-wing left the nest. Its underparts were plucked bare. The remaining plumage differed from that of the adults in the green wings with a few brown feathers on the coverts. A second chick left the nest on August 26; it was badly affected with rickets. Sadly, it died 22 days later.

This taught me a lesson I was never to forget: to inspect all nest-boxes regularly when they contain chicks. That might seem obvious today. In the 1970s the general belief was that if one interfered with the nest the parents would desert. Also the only form of calcium supplementation known was bone meal. That was right at the start of the era in which the breeding of neotropical parrots was to become commonplace.

George Smith's experiences with this species mirrored mine in some respects. In 1974 his female laid two clutches, always of three eggs with three days between each egg. Even before eggs were laid the female would rapidly return to the nest-box if she caught sight of anyone. During the incubation period the male slept outside the nest-box but frequently entered the nest during the day. As had occurred with my pair, the male removed the female's head feathers until her head was bald. He commented:

"The head-preening, once it starts, is rather vigorous, for it breaks off the dark grey tips to the head feathers to leave huge white patches. It may be that this permanent revelation of the underlying white serves to signal to the preening bird that it is becoming too aggressive. If so these white bases to the feathers may serve to inhibit aggression, as does the hidden white nape-patch of broadtailed parrots." (Smith, 1976.)

George Smith's pair hatched chicks; unfortunately they were killed by the male within a day of hatching. His one glimpse of a newly hatched chick showed that it had long white down. He noted that in his female the skin surrounding the eye became "quite glaring red" when she was breeding, that of the male being only slightly more red.

The Bronze-wing is definitely not a suitable species for the beginner. Wild-caught birds proved difficult to breed. Their aviary-bred young are easier. Nevertheless, Bronze-wing ownership requires a degree of experience and a heightened awareness of the needs of nervous birds.

COUNTRIES OF ORIGIN: Venezuela, Colombia, Ecuador and Peru. The proposed sub-species *P. c. cyanescen* is found from southern Colombia to Peru. It is scarce in the latter country.

Habitat: forested areas in the humid foothills up to the cloud forests, usually from 1,400m up to 2,400, sometimes as low as 120m in north of range.

Status: CITES Appendix II. Declining due to loss of habitat.

Dusky Pionus *(Pionus fuscus)*

Meaning of *fuscus*: dark, dusky.

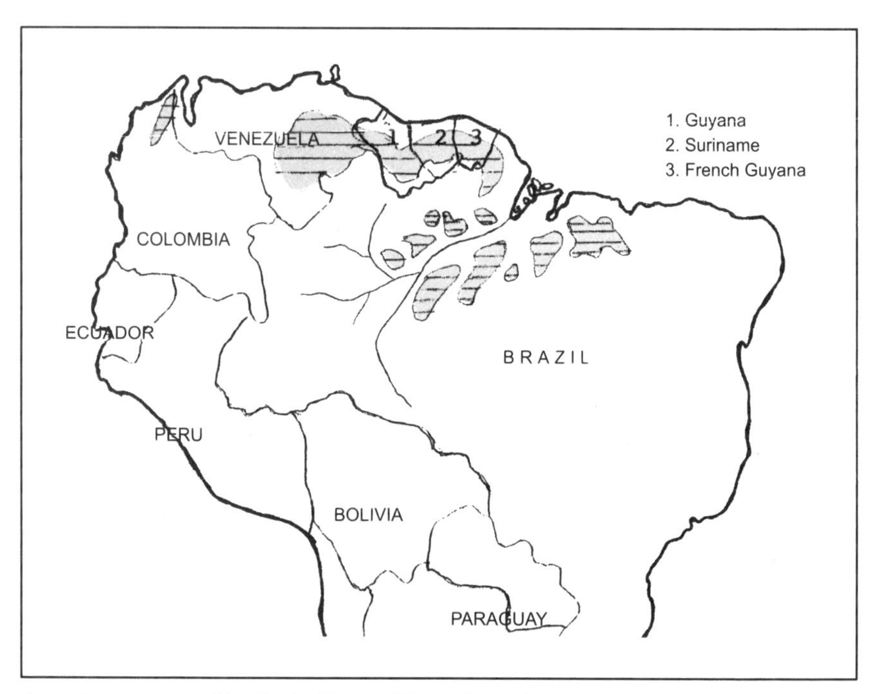

Approximate range of the Dusky Pionus *(Pionus fuscus)*

DISTINGUISHING FEATURES: dark slaty-blue head; the sides of the cere are covered with tiny, dense feathers, usually scarlet, or blue-brown and red. The ear coverts are black. Upperparts are dark brown with paler margins to the feathers. The throat feathers are dark blue tipped with grey or buff. Underparts are variable but generally pinkish-brown, light to dark, rich or pale colours. The beak colour is unusual: dark grey with yellow sides on upper mandible.

Length: 25cm or 26cm (10in).

Weight: about 200g.

IMMATURE BIRDS usually have quite bold head markings, but overall the colours are duller. The skin around the eye is lighter than the grey of adults; the sides of the mandibles are pale yellow, rather than the brighter yellow of adults.

AVICULTURE: Until the late 1970s this was a very rare species in aviculture. Numbers exported from Guyana to Europe increased during the 1980s and 1990s. Unfortunately, mortality among wild--caught birds was extremely high. Most of these birds survived only a few weeks or months, thus although total numbers exported increased, the Dusky has never been a common bird in aviculture. There are now probably more breeding successes than at any other time, but total numbers are not high.

The beautiful and varied coloration attracts some breeders; it seems to be rare for the Dusky to be kept as a companion bird. One breeder recorded that her most colourful male (imported but in captivity for six years) had exceptional wine colour. His first-year offspring were also extraordinary in this respect.

Some birds have the upper breast light pinkish grey. The subtle tones almost defy description. The coloration is highly unusual. The head and upperparts are almost reminiscent of those of a Peregrine Falcon *(Falco peregrinus)*. It is for this reason that the Dusky has sometimes been called "hawk-like" when, of course, it is not. However, its dark head and upperparts and white head feathers with dark shaft- streaking are plumage features which are shared with the Peregrine. Here the resemblance ends. For those who like subtle rather than gaudy coloration in a parrot, the Dusky will have great appeal. Not only does it have a range of muted colours, but these vary in individual birds.

There are no sub-species. It would be interesting to know whether birds from the isolated population in Colombia and Venezuela, separated by at least 1,200km (730 miles) from the main part of the range, differ in their plumage.

The Dusky is not a difficult species to breed; furthermore, it can be prolific. Four or five is the normal clutch size. A friend whose pair normally hatches five young, removes the two eldest for hand-rearing when they reach ringing age, to ensure that the younger chicks receive sufficient food and attention from the parents.

A pair in my care at Loro Parque had their first clutch in 1987 – four infertile eggs. In 1988 the clutch size was again four. There were two eggs by March 1. One egg, probably the last, hatched on April 2. The chick was transferred to a nest of a pair of Maximilian's whose first chick was due to hatch six days later. The chick was found dead the same day. A chick from this clutch that hatched in an incubator also died at one day old so, in both cases, the cause of death might have been pathogenic. Newly hatched chicks have white down which is sparse or fairly sparse. However, another incubator-hatched chick was transferred to the nest of a pair of Coral-billed Pionus who had a newly hatched chick. It was later removed for hand-rearing. At the weaning stage the beak was almost clear pale yellow and the bare skin surrounding the eye was white.

The British breeder John Stoodley recorded a case of nine eggs in one clutch (Stoodley, 1997). Large clutches might be induced by removing the first few eggs in the nest. His female was allowed to keep four eggs as it is difficult for a female to cover more than five. It was not stated how many eggs hatched; some were maintained in a brooder and some in the nest. The chicks were changed around so that the female fed all of them. She had to work hard.

Marie Luise Sandkuhler recorded that her female laid seven eggs, the first on July 29 (Sandkuhler, 1998b). Shortly before they were due to hatch, the female deserted them. The eggs were cold when found. Two chicks hatched but the attempt to hand-rear them from the egg failed. The first egg of the next clutch was laid on March 1 1991. Eleven eggs were laid at three-day intervals! The last appeared on March 31. Eight were fertile. The female was very nervous during incubation and most of the embryos died. One chick hatched but was not fed by the female.

On August 2 the female laid again. Eight eggs were laid. The first and the seventh were infertile and there was a blood ring (indicating early embryo death) in the eighth. On September 10 the third egg had pipped but needed help to hatch. The fourth and fifth eggs hatched on the same day. The last egg contained a fully developed chick that had died. The three chicks weighed 100g when they were ringed with 8.5 mm rings. By 1997 the pair had hatched 14 young.

The second pair was put together in 1993. The male was hatched in Germany in 1988 and the female was wild-caught. Copulation was first observed in October 1993 via closed-circuit television. The first clutch consisted of three fertile eggs. All hatched and the chicks were hand-reared .

In the UK a pair belonging to David Davenport of Cornwall produced their first chicks when they were four years old. They usually nested as early as the end of February or the beginning of March. They were fed supplements containing calcium and Vitamin D just prior to thee start of the breeding season. A piece of 60 mm (1/4in) pine was placed over the front of the nest-box, partially covering the nest entrance. Gnawing their way into the box helped to stimulate the pair to breed. Their first attempt produced five eggs, two of which were fertile. Both hatched. Incubation commenced when the third egg was laid. When the chicks were four weeks old, a tail feather was removed from each chick, for DNA sexing. The young proved to be a male and a female. They left the nest aged about 60 days. The parents then started to roost outside the nest-box, although the young ones roosted inside (Perry, 1997).

COUNTRIES OF ORIGIN: two populations, the main one in Venezuela (eastern), the Guianas and Brazil, and the second on the borders of Colombia and Venezuela.

Habitat: humid tropical evergreen forest, mainly *tierra firma*, but also seasonally flooded forest, also, in the Guianas, savannah woodland and lower highland forest. It shares its range with the Blue-headed Pionus, which far outnumbers it.

Status: CITES Appendix II. It is fairly common but declining in the south and east of its range due to habitat loss.

White-crowned Pionus *(Pionus senilis)*

White-capped Pionus

Meaning of *senilis*: senile – referring to the white crown.

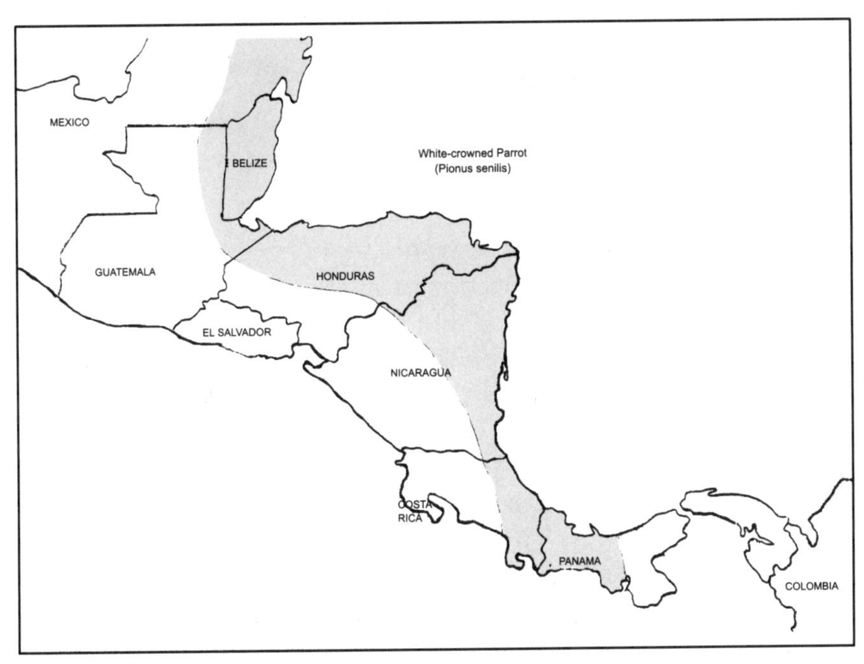

Approximate range of the White-crowned Pionus *(Pionus senilis)*

DISTINGUISHING FEATURES: pure white forehead and crown; small size. Head feathers dark blue with white at the base and green in the centre. Chin and throat are white, sometimes with a few coral-pink feathers. Underparts are dark blue (the feathers have brownish-green centres), merging into blue-green on the abdomen. Wing coverts are bronze and green; primaries are blue. The tail is tipped blue with a red patch near the base. Under tail coverts are red, some with blue margins. The skin around the eye is pink, becoming a deeper shade in breeding condition. The beak is pale yellow.

Length: 24cm (9in).

Weight: about 200g; weight range of 14 birds 166g to 210g (Harcourt-Brown, pers. comm. 1998).

IMMATURE PLUMAGE differs in that:

- The white feathers of the forehead are margined with pink or green.
- The head is mainly green, tinged with black.
- The feathers of the under tail coverts are red and yellow-green.
- The skin surrounding the eye is grey; the beak is yellow marked with grey.

AVICULTURE: When I obtained my first White-crowned Pionus in 1972 it was an avicultural rarity, almost unknown in zoos or trade. This soon altered and this Pionus was exported in quite large numbers from Mexico. The last country to export it was Honduras, up until 1990. Between 1985 and 1990 that country reported the legal export of 6,413. No country within its range now permits its export. Like most Mexican parrots, this species was imported into the USA in large numbers, where it is still quite popular and numerous. However, some birds are quite aggressive and this causes problems for breeders and for pet owners.

This is one of the easier Pionus to persuade to nest. Marie Luise Sandkuhler's pair was first seen in the nest-box in March 1990. The first egg was laid on March 31. The clutch consisted of four fertile eggs. The chicks in the first two eggs died before the yolk sacs were fully absorbed. In the third egg the chick pipped but died after the yolk sac had been absorbed. The chick in the fourth egg also died almost full term. In 1991 the female again laid four fertile eggs. One chick died after pipping the shell. The other three chicks hatched after the nest-box was moistened. The incubation period was 27 days and the chicks weighed 9g, 8g and 7g on hatching. The third chick died on the third day. It had not gained weight. The other two chicks thrived and weighed about 100g when they were ringed. Then the male attacked the female, so he was removed. The weather became very warm (35 deg C or over

95 deg F) and one of the chicks died from heat stress. The other survived after being given fluids.

In 1992 the female again laid four eggs. Aggression between male and female was less violent. The eggs hatched after 27, 25, 26 and 26 days of incubation. The youngest chick was small and died on the fourth day. The other three were reared and proved to be two males and a female. In 1993 the pair did not breed but in December both started to enter the nest. Four fertile eggs were laid at the end of February. The weather was damp. The air space in all four eggs was small. The first, third and fourth eggs hatched after 26, 25 and 23 days. Again, the last chick was small, weighing only 6g on hatching; the other two weighed 8g and 9g. The small chick died but the other two were reared. They proved to be a male and a female. In January 1995 the female laid again. All the young were reared. After they left the nest the male fed them, then mated with the female again. When the young were independent the female laid four more eggs. Only one egg hatched. The chick was a male.

The second pair consisted of a male bred in 1992 and an imported male that had had its flight feathers cut. He aggressively attacked the female. Eventually they mated. The first egg was laid on the ground. The second egg (infertile) was laid in the nest. In 1997 the female laid but did not incubate well. The second egg was placed in an incubator. A chick hatched, weighing 9.8g. It was returned to the nest in the shell. The female brooded it but did not feed it. Mrs Sandkuhler fed the chick then returned it to the nest. She fed it four times a day. On the fifth day it weighed 12.1g. Eventually the female started to feed the chick. It was successfully reared and was first seen to look out of the nest at the end of the ninth week (Sandkuhler, 1998b).

A pair that belonged to Olivier Arnoult first attempted to breed when the female was three years old. Three eggs were laid, reportedly weighing 23g; but this was a misprint and the correct weight was 13g. Two eggs were fertile and the chicks hatched after

26 days. Nest inspection was difficult because both parents were very aggressive. One chick was found dead the day after it hatched; it had been mutilated. The other chick, covered in dense white down on hatching, was well fed. However, it was found dead at 15 days, with a full crop. The female did not enter the nest again that year.

In 1997 the female laid two eggs but only one was fertile. The embryo in the other egg died. The female laid two more eggs in June. Because the pair was so aggressive and nervous, the nest was not inspected during the incubation period. A chick hatched on July 14; the other egg was infertile. All progressed well. The male consumed a lot of fresh corn and germinated seeds. The chick was ringed at 18 days with a 7.5 mm ring. It left the nest at eight weeks. Three weeks later the male attacked the young one. He was therefore removed from his parents. He was spoon-fed each evening for two weeks until he was independent. His coloration was identical to that of his parents except for the lack of white on the forehead which was suffused with a cream colour. The rest of the head and breast were greenish (Arnoult, 1998).

COUNTRIES OF ORIGIN: Mexico, Central America and Panama. It is found mainly on the Caribbean (eastern slope), through Belize, Honduras, Nicaragua and Costa Rica to Panama.

Habitat: a variety of types from humid tropical forest, pine-oak woodland, pine savannah, semi-open and agricultural areas; up to 1,600m or higher, and in cloud forest.

Status: CITES Appendix II. Common and widespread except at edge of range in Panama and in western Nicaragua where it might already be extinct due to loss of habitat.

References cited

Anon, 1997a, Success and failure with Bronze-winged Pionus, *Bird Keeper*, Sept: 4–45.

Anon, 1997b, Life with Maxi's, *Bird Keeper*, Oct: 18–19.

Attrill, R. A., 1991, Breeding Bronzewing Pionus, *Magazine of the Parrot Society*, XXV (1): 10–11.

Arnoult, O., 1998, Pionus a front bleu, *La revue des Oiseaux Exotiques*, No 223 (3): 1–113.

Brockner, A., 1996, Der Schwartzorhpapagei, *Papageien* 9 (9): 269–272.

Collar, N., 1997, in *Handbook of the Birds of the World*, Lynx Edicions, Barcelona.

Cravens, E., 1997, Creative Parrotkeeping, *The Pet Bird Report*, 7 (4): 18–23.

Dorge, R., 1996, Breeding Maximilian's Pionus Parrots, *Bird Breeder*, 68 (5): 31–34.
2001, Aviary Antics, *Parrots*, issue 37: 48–51.

Galetti, M., 1993, Diet of the Scaly-headed Parrot *(Pionus maximiliani)* in a semi- deciduous forest in southeastern Brazil, *Biotropica*, 225 (4): 419–425.

Low, Rosemary, 1972, *The Parrots of South America*, John Gifford, London.
1976, Breeding the Bronze-winged Parrot, *Avicultural Magazine*, 82 (4): 185–189.
1988, Little known about rare Massena's, *Cage & Aviary Birds*, Sept. 10: 14.
1992, *Parrots, their care and breeding* (third ed.), Blandford, London.

McWatters, A., 1996, The Maximilian's Pionus, *Bird Talk*, 14 (12): 28–30, 32, 3.

O'Neill, J. P. and T. A. Parker, 1977, Taxonomy and range of *Pionus "seniloides"* in Peru, *Condor*, 79 (2).

Peck, B., 1988, Bronze Winged Parrot, *Foreign Birds*, 54 (4): 107–109.

Perry, J., 1997, David's Duskys, *Bird Keeper*, Nov: 25–26.

Sandkuhler, M. L., 1998a, Rotsteisspapageien – Freud und Leid, *Papageien* 11 (1): 16–19, and 1998b (part 2) *Papageien*, 11 (2): 44–48.

Sick, H., 1993, *Birds in Brazil*, Princeton University Press, New Jersey.

Smith, G., [No title], *Avicultural Magazine*, 82 (4): 189–190.

Stoodley, J., 1978, The breeding of four species of Pionus, *Avicultural Magazine*, 84 (2): 62–64.
1997, The Dusky Parrots, *Just Parrots and Parrakeets*, issue 14: 16–18.

Sweeney, R., 1997a, Success of Loro Parque strategy, *Cage & Aviary Birds*, Nov 15: 10.
1997b, Blue-headed Pionus – the 'peck'able pet Parrot, *Cage & Aviary Birds*, Dec: 13:14.

Tell, M., 1983, Breeding the Siy Parrot, *Avicultural Magazine*, 89 (1): 27–29.

Worth, G., 1997, Maximilian's longevity, *Bird Talk*, 15 (7): 90–91.

Pionus Parrots

Published, printed and bound in the Czech Republic by
DONA Publishing, Komenského 37, 370 01 České Budějovice.
Photos: Rosemary Low.
Design: Jiří Jabulka.

ISBN 80-7322-005-9